D1522711

UNBROKEN: TURNING PAIN INTO PURPOSE

JUAN ESPINOZA

CONTENTS

THIS BOOK IS FOR

This book is for anyone who has ever felt the weight of life's challenges and wondered if they'd ever find the strength to rise again. This book is for fighters who have been knocked down but refused to stay there, dreamers striving to turn visions into reality, and survivors who wear their pain as a badge of resilience. It's for those who've faced loss, heartbreak, failure, and betrayal yet found a way to keep moving forward.

To the soldier returning home, navigating a world that feels foreign after the chaos of war—this book is for you. I understand what it's like to return to a life that has moved on without you, to wrestle with memories that linger and scars that take longer to heal than you'd hoped. It's for the parents tirelessly working to provide for their children, sacrificing time, energy, and parts of themselves to create a brighter future. For those who've loved deeply and lost but dared to open their hearts again, this book is yours.

It's for anyone carrying the wounds of their past into their present, grappling with forgiving themselves for mistakes made when they didn't know better. It's for those who've tried to fit someone else's mold only to discover that living authentically is the only way forward. For anyone learning that forgiveness—whether for others or themselves—is not weakness but a declaration of strength and a step toward peace.

This book is for the ones who understand the fight required to build a better life, even when the odds seem impossible. Whether you've biked miles to work to provide for your family, stood amidst the ruins of a broken marriage searching for a way to rebuild, or burned the midnight oil chasing a dream that feels just out of reach—this book is for you.

This book is for the fighters, the dreamers, and anyone who has felt pain they thought they couldn't bear. It's for those who turned struggles into stepping stones, failures into wisdom, and losses into legacies. My story isn't perfect—it's messy, raw, and real. It's about resilience, forgiveness, and learning to rise, no matter how many times life knocks you down.

As you read these pages, I hope you find something that resonates—a lesson, a moment, or simply a reminder that you're not alone. This book isn't just about my journey; it's about yours too. Life will test you, but those tests are opportunities to uncover your strength, purpose, and power.

To anyone who's ever felt broken, questioned their worth, or wondered if they could keep going—this book is for you. I hope my story reminds you of your capability. You are stronger than your pain, greater than your mistakes, and worthy of love and peace.

So, as you step into the next chapter of your life, remember: you're not defined by your struggles but by how you rise from them. Embrace the chaos, find peace in the storm, and never stop fighting for the life you deserve. Your story matters—write it boldly, authentically, unapologetically.

This book is for you. Thank you for being part of my journey. Keep fighting, keep growing, and never lose sight of your incredible strength. Together, let's redefine what it means to rise, love, and live fully.

CHAPTER 1

Laying the Foundation Every Journey Starts Somewhere

Every journey has a starting point, and mine began in a modest home where love and struggle coexisted in equal measure. It wasn't a grand beginning—no sprawling estates or picture-perfect family portraits—just something real. A home where resilience was built into the walls and love, even if imperfectly expressed, held everything together.

As a child, the world felt like an endless playground. The sidewalks of my neighborhood weren't just paths; they were race tracks for my bike, canvases for chalk art, and proving grounds for games we invented on the spot. Every nook and cranny of the backyard seemed to hold a secret, waiting to be discovered.

I spent my days climbing trees, racing down uneven sidewalks, and dreaming of far-off places where anything seemed possible.

I imagined myself as an explorer charting unknown territories or a superhero saving the day—the kind of fantasies only childhood allows you to believe without question. My biggest concerns were whether my mom would call me in for dinner before I was ready or if my friends could come out to play. Life lessons were there, simmering beneath the surface, but I was too busy exploring, imagining, and simply living to notice them.

Looking back, I see now that those carefree days weren't just play— they were the foundation of who I'd become. Even in the smallest moments, life was shaping me, preparing me for challenges I couldn't yet imagine. Scraped knees taught me that healing takes time and effort. Losing a race showed me the value of persistence. And the long summer days of endless curiosity revealed the joy found in hard work and determination.

Childhood has a way of teaching lessons quietly. Falling from a tree taught me to climb more carefully. Watching my hours of work building a fort blown away by the wind forced me to turn frustration into creativity as I rebuilt it stronger. When my bike hit a rock and sent me flying, I learned to get back up, dust myself off, and keep pedaling. Life, in its subtle way, was showing me that setbacks weren't endings but stepping stones to something greater.

But it wasn't just fun and games that shaped me—home struggles had their role, too. We didn't have much, but we made do with what we had. My parents worked tirelessly to provide for us, often sacrificing their own needs. I didn't understand the depth of those sacrifices then, but I felt their determination in their tired smiles at the end of long days. Love in our house wasn't always spoken—it was shown. It was in the meals cooked; the lights kept on, and the whispered encouragement during moments of doubt. These quiet

acts of love planted seeds of gratitude and resilience in me that
would bloom later in life.

Life at that time wasn't perfect, but it was real. It was in that
imperfect home, surrounded by imperfect people, that I learned
the importance of caring for others. The lessons my parents taught
me—both intentionally and through their actions—helped me
understand the value of showing up for the people you love, even
when it's hard.

Looking back, my childhood was a delicate balance of joy and
struggle. The scraped knees were just as important as the laughter-
filled days with my siblings. It was all part of a bigger picture—a
quiet preparation for the storms I would face later in life. Resilience,
persistence, and gratitude were forged during those early years,
even when I didn't realize it at the time.

▌ REFLECTIVE PAUSE:

- **What moments from your childhood felt carefree but
  taught you something deeper?**
- **What lessons were hidden in the simplest moments of
  play or struggle?**
- **How did the sacrifices of the people around you shape
  who you've become?**

Sometimes, the foundation of who we are doesn't come from
monumental events but from small, meaningful moments—the
playful days, tough lessons, and sacrifices we never fully understood
until we looked back. What are the foundations of your journey?
What stories do you carry with you?

3

A HOME BUILT ON SACRIFICE

Growing up, we weren't rich—not even close. But my parents, despite their imperfections, built a foundation of love and sacrifice that shaped who I am today. Our home was simple, a modest sanctuary that reflected our struggles, but it was also filled with invaluable lessons about hard work, perseverance, and the unwavering importance of family.

My dad worked long, grueling hours at a physically demanding job. He'd leave before the sun rose and return long after it had set, his hands calloused and his body worn from the day. As a child, I didn't fully grasp the weight of his sacrifices. To me, he was just Dad—the man who told corny jokes, hoisted me onto his shoulders when I was too tired to walk, and seemed invincible. But as I grew older, the depth of his commitment to our family became clear.

I vividly remember one particularly harsh winter when our heater broke. The cold crept into every corner of the house, but my dad didn't complain or panic. Instead, he found an old space heater at a garage sale and moved it from room to room each night, ensuring we stayed warm. It wasn't the perfect solution, but it worked. That was my dad's way—he didn't dwell on what we didn't have; he focused on making the best of what we did.

Christmases were humble but full of meaning. Our tiny Christmas tree, no more than a foot tall, stood on a corner table, with just a handful of presents underneath. As a child, I didn't focus on what we lacked. Now, as an adult, I see those small Christmases for what they truly were: monumental acts of love. My parents worked tirelessly to give us the best life they could, even if it meant sacrificing their own comforts. As a kid, I didn't understand the

4

weight of their efforts, but today, I hold deep appreciation for those seemingly small acts of love.

My mom was the glue that held our family together. Her sacrifices were quieter but no less significant. She was the unseen force behind every family meal, every clean shirt, and every comforting hug when the world felt too overwhelming. I remember seeing her skip meals so we'd have enough to eat or wear the same pair of worn-out shoes for years because she prioritized our needs over her own.

One day after school, I came home to find my mom sitting with one of my sisters, carefully fixing her favorite dress. My sister had torn it while playing, and though it was just a piece of clothing, I could see how much it meant to her. My mom's hands moved methodically, stitching it back together as though it were brand new.

It wasn't just about mending the dress; it was the lesson embedded in the act. My mom wasn't simply repairing fabric—she was showing us the importance of care, resourcefulness, and valuing what we had. When my sister proudly wore the dress again, her joy was undeniable, and my mom's quiet satisfaction spoke volumes. Moments like these revealed my mom's true character: a woman who poured love into every action, no matter how big or small.

Looking back, I realize how these seemingly ordinary moments defined my parents and the values they instilled in us. My dad taught us resilience and the value of hard work. My mom taught us compassion, resourcefulness, and how to meet challenges with grace. Together, they showed us that love doesn't have to be loud

5

or extravagant—it often lies in quiet sacrifices and meaningful acts of care.

These lessons have stayed with me, shaping how I approach challenges, relationships, and gratitude. They've taught me that love isn't about perfection—it's about presence and intention. Through their sacrifices, my parents gave me the tools to navigate life with purpose and an appreciation for what truly matters.

▌ REFLECTIVE PAUSE:

- **Who in your family made sacrifices for you, and how have those sacrifices shaped your life?**
- **What small but meaningful moments of love from your family stand out to you now?**
- **How have the acts of care and resourcefulness you witnessed influenced the way you live your life?**

▌ A MOTHER'S LOVE

The mother who raised me wasn't my biological mother; she was my stepmom. But in every way that mattered, she was my real mom. She entered our lives when I was just three years old, at a time when my sister and I desperately needed stability and love. She didn't just marry my dad—she chose us, too. With unwavering commitment, she filled the void my biological mother had left, giving us the kind of love and care that can only come from a heart dedicated to healing and nurturing.

I'll never forget the first time I called her "**Mom**." It felt natural, almost casual at the time, but the look on her face told me it was anything but. Her eyes welled up with tears, and in that moment, I realized how much it meant to her. She wasn't just stepping into a role—she was stepping into our lives with open arms and an open heart. She didn't love us out of obligation; she loved us because she chose to.

Life hadn't been easy for her, and she carried her own scars—some visible, others hidden deep within. But she never let those scars stop her from being kind and generous with her love. She wasn't perfect—no one is—but she was perfect for us. She taught me the true meaning of unconditional love: to care for someone not because you have to, but because you truly want to.

Her personality was fierce and unapologetic. She had a presence that could shake the walls of a room. When she raised her voice, everyone paid attention. My mom was known for her fiery temper, and when she was upset, whatever was within reach might go flying across the room. A coffee cup in one hand and a cigarette in the other were her trademarks. She was proudly Native American, and if you didn't know it, she'd make sure you did. She never sugarcoated her words, and if she didn't like you, she'd tell you to your face without hesitation.

I loved pushing her buttons, even if it meant risking her wrath. She'd call it "**raising her blood pressure**," and we'd go back and forth, me testing her patience and her reminding me exactly who was in charge. But through every fiery argument and no-nonsense lecture, I never doubted her love. She didn't just tell me she loved me; she showed it, in ways that words alone could never express.

In contrast, my biological mother's absence painted a much different picture. She left when we were young, and the memories

7

I have of her are scattered, tinged with confusion and pain. One memory, in particular, stands out vividly: a night spent sleeping in a car parked behind a dumpster after she'd had an argument with a man. At the time, I didn't fully understand what was happening, but that moment told me everything about her priorities. The pain from her choices ran deep, but it also gave me clarity about the kind of love I wanted—and deserved—in my life.

My stepmom didn't just fill the void my biological mother left; she redefined what it meant to be a parent. Through her own strength, she taught me resilience. Through her fierce, protective love, she gave me a foundation I didn't realize I needed until much later in life.

She may not have given birth to me, but she gave me everything else: her time, her energy, her wisdom, and her unwavering commitment. For that, I will always be grateful. She didn't just step into a role; she transformed our lives.

▌ REFLECTIVE PAUSE:

- Was there someone in your life who stepped in to love or support you in an unexpected way?
- How has their influence shaped the person you are today?
- What does it mean to you when someone chooses to love, even when they don't have to?

▌A FATHER'S LESSONS

My dad was a man of few words, but his actions spoke louder than any lecture ever could. Growing up in a foreign country, his tough childhood taught him the value of hard work, perseverance, and resilience. For him, failure wasn't an option, and he passed that belief on to me—not through lengthy speeches or advice, but through the quiet power of example.

One of my most vivid memories of him is from a camping trip when I was about five years old. I was playing near the campfire when my dad casually tossed a rock out of the flames. In my childlike curiosity, I thought it was a ball and grabbed it with my bare hands. The pain was immediate and excruciating, and my screams echoed through the woods. My dad, ever resourceful, sprang into action. Without hesitation, he wrapped my burned hands in napkins and duct tape. It wasn't the most elegant solution, but it worked. That moment wasn't just about treating a burn— it was a lesson in adaptability and resourcefulness. From that day forward, I understood that when faced with a problem, you don't waste time complaining or overthinking—you solve it with whatever tools you have.

My father wasn't perfect, but he was steadfast in his own way. He was a man who helped family and others quietly, without seeking recognition. He carried his burdens privately, never letting us see the full extent of his struggles. But even as a child, I could see the subtle signs—his tired eyes, the way his shoulders slumped at the end of a long day. He bore his pain alone, not out of pride, but to shield us from worry.

9

My dad was incredibly creative and skilled with his hands. I remember watching him turn raw pieces of metal into beautifully crafted knives, transforming old wrenches into gleaming blades. He could take a fallen tree and turn it into a magnificent table. He'd cut down the tree himself, slice the wood into slabs, and craft furniture that belonged in a showroom. He was an artist, though he'd never call himself that. His craftsmanship wasn't about seeking accolades—it was about creating something meaningful and lasting.

His work ethic was unmatched. He worked tirelessly, rain or shine, often tackling the toughest projects in the worst weather. I'd warn him, **"Dad, you know it's going to rain, right?"** He didn't care. He'd press on, dragging me along to help. Whether we were repairing a fence or hauling wood in a downpour, his attitude was always the same: the job didn't stop because it's inconvenient.

Working alongside my dad became a weekend tradition. Whether it was fixing a broken lawnmower, patching a leaky roof, or clearing out a clogged drain, his mantra was always the same: **"You don't quit until it's done."** At the time, I thought he was just being tough on me, pushing me harder than necessary. But now, I see that he was preparing me for life. He was teaching me resilience and self-reliance—lessons that have carried me through some of my hardest moments.

The truth is, my dad's lessons weren't just about fixing things—they were about fixing yourself when life tries to break you. He taught me that resilience isn't about pretending to be unshakable; it's about getting back up every time you're knocked down. He didn't preach about grit—he lived it. And by working alongside him, I absorbed it.

His quiet strength and relentless determination are with me to this day. I still think about the times he worked in the pouring rain, not because he had to, but because he chose to. He taught me that perseverance isn't something you turn on and off—it's a way of life. And now, when I face challenges, I hear his voice in my head, telling me to keep going, to find a solution, and to never, ever quit.

▌ REFLECTIVE PAUSE:

- **What lessons about grit and resilience did you learn from your parents or caregivers?**
- **Can you think of a time when you faced a tough situation and found a way to solve it?**
- **How have those lessons shaped the way you approach challenges today?**

I was the only boy in a family of four kids, surrounded by three sisters: Amanda, Kat, and D. Each of them influenced my life in unique ways, shaping the person I am today. Their presence gave me a deeper understanding of love, sacrifice, and resilience. Each sister brought something different to the table, and together, their collective impact on my life is immeasurable.

D, my oldest sister, and I weren't as close due to family dynamics and the complexities of life. Yet, no matter the distance or differences between us, the bond of family remains unshaken. She is still my sister, and that's something that doesn't change.

▌ AMANDA: THE STRENGTH OF SACRIFICE

Amanda, my older sister, was a constant source of strength and wisdom. Her quiet determination in the face of adversity was something I deeply admired. Amanda inherited much of my mom's fierce personality, and though her heart often carried burdens, it was always filled with love. She has a fiery side to her that you didn't want to see. The same personality as my Mom so they clashed a lot. I remember the screaming matches Amanda had with my mom when I was young.

Giving up was never an option for her. Amanda worked tirelessly to provide for her family, taking on responsibilities that no teenager should have to bear. When we were younger, she often took on a caregiver role, watching over me and Kat when our parents weren't around. It wasn't a choice she made, but a duty thrusted upon her, one she carried with resilience and love.

Looking back, I now realize how much Amanda's teenage years were shaped by the sacrifices she made. While her peers enjoyed their youth, Amanda stayed home, ensuring we were safe and cared for. I remember sneaking out of bed late at night to find her asleep on the couch, MTV softly playing in the background. I'd creep in to watch the videos, knowing I wasn't supposed to, but it was those moments that made me appreciate her quiet strength.

As the years passed, Amanda continued to hold us together, especially after our mom passed away. She became the glue of our family—organizing dinners, checking in on us, and always being there when we needed someone to talk to. As I got older, I believed I could outdrink her, but she proved me wrong by putting me under the table. I remember waking up on the couch and she was eating a snack watching tv like nothing phased her. As I've grown older have I truly come to understand and appreciate the magnitude of her sacrifices. For everything she's done, and does for me, I'll always be grateful.

▌ KAT: THE MIRROR AND THE OPPOSITE

Kat, my twin sister, was both my mirror and my opposite. While I was impulsive and carefree, she was disciplined and methodical. Together, we created a balance that was as unbreakable as it was unique.

We were yin and yang—complementary in every way. Kat's resilience and determination were inspiring, and she constantly reminded me that failure is not the end; it's merely a stepping stone. Our childhood was filled with mischief and adventures. I'll never forget the time we were riding in the back of our dad's truck on a dirt road during a camping trip. Kat dared me to jump out and run alongside the moving truck. Always the daredevil, I accepted the challenge, convinced I could pull it off. **SPOILER ALERT**: I couldn't. I hit the ground hard and rolled, my dad slamming on the brakes as chaos unfolded in the rearview mirror. As he helped me back into the truck, battered and bruised, he simply said, "**Did you learn your lesson? Now get in.**"

Kat and I were opposites in other ways, too. Growing up, she would always come home and do her homework for hours and I never had any since I did it in class, but our grades showed that I was full of it. She has a free-spirited hippie side that clashed with me being more grounded and analytical. I teased her relentlessly, like the time she told me that certain days were better for getting vitamin

13

D from the sun. I laughed, insisting that sunlight was sunlight—it didn't make a difference. She rolled her eyes, probably thinking I was crazy. But as I've grown older, I've come to admire her open-mindedness and her willingness to seek her own truth, even when it meant taking an unconventional path. We are all similar where we don't try to worry each other with our burdens, but we can tell if we are hurting.

LESSONS FROM GROWING UP WITH SISTERS

Growing up with sisters taught me patience, empathy, and the importance of showing up for the people you love. Amanda showed me the power of sacrifice and resilience. Kat taught me the beauty of balance and the value of forging your own path. And even though distance exists between me and D, I've learned that family bonds persist across time and space. I provide a wild side to this mix where I'm ready for anything. They call me crazy, but that's just me.

My sisters weren't just my first friends—they were my first teachers. They showed me how to navigate life's complexities with love, strength, and grace. Their impact on my life is something words can never fully capture, but it's a gift I carry with me every day. For that, I'll always be grateful.

REFLECTIVE PAUSE:

- **If you have siblings, how have they influenced your life?**

- What lessons have you learned from your family relationships?
- In what ways have the sacrifices of your siblings or family members shaped your perspective on life?

Looking back on my childhood, I see it as a tapestry woven with threads of love, sacrifice, resilience, and growth. Each moment, whether joyous or challenging, added a unique blend to my upbringing. My parents and siblings weren't just family—they were my first teachers, and the lessons they imparted became the foundation upon which I built my character.

Childhood wasn't perfect. There were struggles that weighed heavily on us, moments that forced us to grow before we were ready, and sacrifices made quietly in the background. Yet, those imperfections were rich with lessons that prepared me for the journey ahead. They taught me to find strength in adversity, to value hard work, and to never take love for granted.

THE STRENGTH IN ADVERSITY

Adversity has a way of shaping people, and for my family, it was a constant companion. My parents worked tirelessly to provide for us. My dad, with his calloused hands and weary body, taught me the importance of perseverance. He never complained about the long hours or harsh conditions of his work. Instead, he faced each challenge with quiet determination, showing me that strength isn't loud or boastful—it's steady and unwavering.

My mom's sacrifices, though quieter, were just as impactful. She made sure we had food on the table, even if it meant skipping meals herself. She wore the same shoes for years, so we could have what we needed. Her love wasn't flashy, but it was steadfast and selfless, a reminder that real love is about putting others before yourself.

From these examples, I learned that strength isn't about avoiding hardships; it's about facing them head-on and finding a way through. I began to see adversity not as something to fear, but as an opportunity to grow and prove to myself what I was capable of overcoming.

Growing up in a modest home meant that nothing was handed to us. If we wanted something, we had to earn it. Watching my dad work long hours taught me the dignity of labor. He didn't give lectures on responsibility—he led by example, showing us that hard work wasn't just a necessity; it was a virtue.

On weekends, I joined him on his projects. Whether we were repairing a fence or building something from scratch, he made sure I understood the value of persistence. His mantra was simple: **"If you're going to do something, do it right the first time."** Those words stuck with me, shaping how I approached challenges at every stage of life.

My siblings also demonstrated the value of hard work in their own ways. Amanda, my older sister, took on responsibilities far beyond her years, stepping into a caregiver role when our parents were busy. She taught me that hard work wasn't just about physical effort—it was also about emotional strength, showing up for others, and being a steady presence in their lives.

If there's one thing my childhood taught me, it's that love isn't just an emotion—it's an action. My parents showed their love through sacrifices, hard work, and unwavering support. Even in difficult times, they found ways to make us feel cared for and valued.

My mom had a gift for turning small moments into something meaningful. Whether it was mending a torn dress or comforting me after a rough day, her actions spoke volumes. She taught me that love isn't always about grand gestures—it's about being there, consistently and wholeheartedly.

My siblings, too, were constant reminders of love's power. They were my first friends, confidants, and partners in crime. Even when we fought, as siblings do, I always knew they had my back. Their unwavering loyalty taught me the importance of maintaining strong connections with those who matter the most.

Childhood struggles have a way of imprinting lessons that last a lifetime. For me, those struggles taught me to appreciate what I had and to make the most of every opportunity. They instilled resilience—the ability to bounce back from setbacks and keep moving forward.

I learned that setbacks aren't failures; they're stepping stones. Falling from a tree taught me persistence. Losing a race taught me humility. Every struggle, no matter how small, added to my understanding of life's complexities and prepared me for the challenges to come.

REFLECTING ON RESILIENCE

Resilience, to me, is the ability to face adversity without letting it break you. It's not about being unshakable; it's about getting back up, time and time again. My understanding of resilience comes from watching my parents and siblings navigate life's challenges with grace and determination.

I see resilience in my dad, who kept going even when he was exhausted. I saw it in my mom, who created warmth and stability despite limited resources. I see it in my siblings, who stepped up and took on responsibilities far beyond their years.

These examples didn't just teach me how to survive—they taught me how to thrive. They showed me that challenges are opportunities in disguise and that true strength is about transforming pain into growth.

As I transitioned into adulthood, I carried these lessons with me, ready to face whatever challenges life had in store. Little did I know, the next chapter would test me in ways I couldn't have imagined.

Adulthood brought its own struggles—some predictable, others unexpected. But through it all, I leaned on the foundation my childhood had given me. Resilience, hard work, and an appreciation for love and sacrifice became my guiding principles.

Looking back, I realize that my childhood wasn't perfect, but it was exactly what I needed to prepare myself for the journey ahead. Every challenge, every lesson, every act of love—it all shaped me into who I am today. Through those imperfections, it helped me realize that life isn't perfect, but if you see the beauty of those imperfections, you will see the real meaning in life and what it has to teach us.

▌REFLECTIVE PAUSE:

- **What moments shaped your childhood?**
- **What lessons did you learn from the people around you, the struggles you faced, or the dreams you chased?**
- **How do you define resilience, and where did that understanding come from?**

These questions invite us to look back and find meaning in our experiences. They remind us that even in struggle, there is growth. And they challenge us to carry those lessons forward, using them as a compass for the journey ahead.

CHAPTER 2

The Military Years-
Strength Forged in Chaos

Joining the military wasn't a spur-of-the-moment decision, nor was it born out of desperation. It was a deliberate choice—a calculated step toward finding purpose and reshaping my future. By the time I graduated high school, my options felt limited. I hadn't taken my education seriously, and my grades reflected that. Scholarships weren't an option, and my parents couldn't afford to send me to college. The idea of settling into a mundane 9-to-5 job felt suffocating. I craved something more—something that would challenge me, force me to grow, and give my life direction.

Growing up, I always felt a pull toward something bigger—something that would allow me to prove myself and earn respect. I wasn't content with just existing; I wanted to make an impact, to push myself beyond what I thought I was capable of. The military offered that opportunity—a chance to redefine myself, to leave behind the kid who didn't take school seriously and become someone I could be proud of.

When I announced my decision to enlist, the reactions from my family were mixed. My parents, though supportive in their quiet way, were worried. They understood the dangers and struggled to accept my choice. My dad, a man of few words, simply nodded when I told him, but I could see the concern in his eyes—the unspoken fear of losing his son. My aunt, on the other hand, was more direct. "**I'll take out a life insurance policy on you because you're going to die**," she said bluntly. Her words stung, but I knew they came from a place of love and fear. It was 2009, and the war in Afghanistan was raging. Enlisting in the infantry meant stepping directly into the line of fire, and survival wasn't guaranteed.

Despite their fears, I was resolute. This was my choice, and I was determined to see it through. I walked into the recruiter's office with clear intentions. "**I want to join**," I said. When they asked me what I wanted to do, my answer was simple: "**I want to be in the fight**." Without hesitation, they offered me the job of infantryman, and I accepted without a second thought. I signed on the dotted line, fully aware of the challenges and risks ahead.

THE WEIGHT OF THE DECISION

Looking back, I realize how significant that decision was. At the time, it felt like a way out of a stagnant life, but it was so much more than that. It was the first step in a journey that would shape my character, test my resilience, and teach me lessons no classroom or textbook ever could.

The military didn't just give me a job—it gave me a sense of purpose. It provided structure, discipline, and a mission to focus on. It filled a void I hadn't even realized was there. But with purpose came responsibility, and with responsibility came fear. The thought of going to war, of facing life-and-death situations, was terrifying, but it was also exhilarating. It was the kind of fear that pushes you to grow, to become better and stronger.

My family's reactions stayed with me. My parents, though initially silent, eventually found ways to support me. My mom slipped notes into my bag—small reminders of home that I'd discover during challenging days in training. My dad, though stoic, told me he was proud of me in the moments that mattered most.

My aunt's blunt words were harder to shake. While her statement wasn't meant to discourage me, it reminded me of the gravity of my decision. She wasn't wrong—there was a very real risk involved. But her words also fueled my determination. They became a reminder of what I was stepping into and a source of motivation to prove, to myself and to my family, that I could rise to the challenge.

THE FIRST STEP

Boarding the plane to Fort Benning, Georgia, was a surreal experience. Looking out the window as the plane ascended, I felt a mix of emotions. I was leaving behind the familiar—home, family, and the person I used to be. The kid who lacked direction, who didn't take school seriously—that version of me was staying behind.

When the plane touched down in Georgia, excitement and apprehension surged within me. Basic training loomed ahead, a

22

gauntlet of physical and mental challenges designed to strip away the old and forge the new. I wasn't looking for an easy path—I was seeking transformation.

Joining the military wasn't just about finding direction—it was about becoming part of something bigger than myself. It was about serving a purpose, contributing to a mission, and being part of a team that relied on each other to succeed. I wanted to test my limits and prove to myself that I could rise to the occasion when it mattered most.

At its core, my decision to join the military was about transformation. It was about stepping out of the shadows of complacency and stepping into a role that demanded discipline, courage, and resilience. It was about finding out who I truly was and what I was capable of.

The journey was just beginning, but even in those early days, I knew I had made the right choice. The path ahead wouldn't be easy, but it would be worth it. Every challenge, every obstacle, and every moment of doubt would serve a purpose. It would shape me, mold me, and prepare me for the road ahead.

As I stepped off that plane and into the next chapter of my life, I carried with me the hopes and fears of my family, the lessons of my past, and the determination to create a future that mattered. Joining the military wasn't just a decision—it was a declaration. A promise to myself to never settle, to always strive for more, and to embrace the challenges that would ultimately define me.

REFLECTIVE PAUSE:

- **What moments in your life marked the beginning of a significant transformation?**
- **How do fear and purpose coexist when making life-changing decisions?**
- **In what ways have challenges shaped your understanding of who you are?**

These questions invite us to examine the pivotal moments that shape our lives. They remind us that transformation often begins with a decision—a choice to embrace the unknown and pursue something greater than ourselves.

BASIC TRAINING–BREAKING DOWN TO BUILD UP

Fort Benning: A World Away Fort Benning, Georgia, infamous for its relentless infantry basic training, was nothing like the life I left behind in California. From the moment I stepped off the bus, reality hit me like a freight train. There was no easing into it, no time to prepare for what was ahead. Drill sergeants descended on us like hawks, barking orders and stripping away any individuality. Their sharp voices echoed through the air, setting the tone for the weeks to come. Their mission wasn't just to train us, but to break us down completely—to erase who we were and rebuild us as soldiers.

From the first day, the demands were unrelenting. Standing at parade rest for what felt like an eternity introduced us to the military's unforgiving standards. My legs trembled, my back ached, and sweat dripped down my face as Georgia's oppressive humidity clung to me like a wet blanket. Coming from the dry heat of California, I was unprepared for the suffocating air that made even breathing feel like a chore.

The days blurred together in a cycle of grueling physical training, weapons drills, tactical exercises, and constant shouting. Sleep became a luxury, with only a few hours each night to recover before the next round of challenges. Meals were rushed, eaten with urgency, and devoid of comfort. Some recruits cracked under the pressure, leaving gaps in the ranks as the rest of us pressed on.

For those of us who stayed, the bonds we formed became our lifeline. The shared hardships created a camaraderie unlike anything I'd ever experienced. Together, we endured punishing drills, endless runs, and the constant demands of our drill sergeants. Crawling through mud under barbed wire, running miles in full gear, and struggling to stay awake during late-night classes became shared experiences that tied us together.

These moments built a trust that was deeper than friendship—it was a brotherhood forged in sweat, grit, and determination. We leaned on each other in the hardest moments, knowing that success depended on our ability to work as a team.

The most defining moment of basic training came at the end: the final ruck march. This was no ordinary march—it was a 12-mile trek with 45-pound packs, a grueling test of endurance and mental strength. Each step felt like a battle as the weight dug into my shoulders and my legs screamed in protest. The route seemed endless, the hills steeper with every mile, and exhaustion hung over us like a storm cloud.

Reaching the finish line felt like a miracle. My body was on the verge of collapse, my lungs burned, and my feet were raw. But what awaited us made every step worthwhile. Flames roared from the towering walls, casting an intense glow over the scene, while heavy metal music blasted through the air. Drill sergeants stood at attention, waiting with our infantry badges.

The ceremony was surreal, almost cult-like in its fervor. When the badge was pinned to my chest, it wasn't done gently. The drill sergeant delivered a hard punch, driving the pins into my skin. The sharp sting was a reminder of what I had endured to earn it. In that moment, pride and accomplishment overwhelmed me. I had survived, and I had earned my place.

101ST AIRBORNE 1/327 "ABOVE THE REST"

Joining the 101st Airborne In December 2009, I graduated from basic training and returned home for a brief Christmas break. Seeing my family felt surreal. After weeks of relentless training, the comforts of home—like a warm bed and quiet nights—felt foreign. But I knew this reprieve wouldn't last.

By January 2010, I was on my way to my first unit: the 101st Airborne Division, 1st Battalion, 327th Infantry Regiment, known as "Above the Rest." The 101st Airborne's history of heroism and sacrifice was legendary, and joining its ranks felt like stepping into a military epic. Any romantic notions I had about the unit quickly faded. **"Basic training means nothing here,"** our leaders made clear. **"We'll teach you the real way."** They weren't lying.

Mornings began before dawn with long runs, or ruck marches, sometimes stretching 20 miles. Rain, snow, or blistering heat—

it didn't matter. We trained in all conditions, pushing through exhaustion and adapting to every challenge. The rest of the day was spent perfecting marksmanship, running tactical drills, or participating in field exercises that often lasted for weeks. Sleep deprivation became routine, blurring the line between reality and hallucination.

One training exercise in Colorado stands out vividly in my memory. We had been awake for 36 hours straight, running missions and manning defensive positions. As fatigue set in, my mind began to play tricks on me. While manning a fighting position, I thought I saw a face in a pile of leaves. My heart raced, adrenaline surging as I prepared to act—but it was nothing more than a hallucination. That moment reminded me of the limits of the human body and mind and the importance of relying on training when exhaustion takes over.

Lessons Learned from basic training and my early days with the 101st Airborne taught me lessons that would last a lifetime.

Discipline: The value of doing things the right way, every time, no matter how tired or overwhelmed you feel.

Perseverance: The strength to push forward when every part of you wants to stop.

Camaraderie: The power of shared struggles to create unbreakable bonds.

More than anything, I learned resilience. Every challenge, every obstacle, and every moment of doubt was an opportunity to grow stronger. Basic training didn't just prepare me for combat—it prepared me for life. It taught me that no matter how tough things get, there's always a way forward—and that the bonds formed in hardship can carry you through anything.

▌ REFLECTIVE PAUSE:

- **How have moments of intense challenge shaped your sense of resilience?**
- **What lessons have you learned from working as part of a team during difficult times?**
- **How do you push forward when every fiber of your being tells you to stop?**

These experiences remind us that the hardest moments in life are often the ones that teach us the most about ourselves. They push us to grow, to connect, and to discover the strength we didn't know we had.

▌ DEPLOYMENT TO AFGHANISTAN–A JOURNEY INTO CHAOS

Nothing could have truly prepared me for my first deployment to Afghanistan in 2010. At just 18 years old, I was thrust into a war zone where every day was a battle for survival, and every decision carried the weight of life or death. The moment I landed, the gravity of war transformed from an abstract concept into an all-consuming reality. It wasn't just about tactics and strategy; it was a crash course in resilience, fear, and the raw power of human will.

In May 2010, I deployed to Afghanistan's Pech River Valley, Kunar Province, one of the most volatile regions in the country. The rugged terrain and narrow valleys offered endless opportunities for ambushes, while the locals were caught in the crossfire, torn between Taliban control and supporting us. The moment I landed, the gravity of war transformed from an abstract concept into an all-consuming reality. It wasn't just about tactics and strategy; it was a crash course in resilience, fear, and the raw power of human will.

We arrived in Afghanistan aboard a Chinook helicopter under the cover of night, heading straight into the heart of the Pech River Valley. The valleys with towering mountains were both awe-inspiring in their beauty and oppressive in their constant threat of danger. Our base sat right in the pech river valley at the meeting point of the infamous Korengal Valley, one of the deadliest battlegrounds for U.S. forces.

Touching down at Combat Outpost (COP) Michigan, chaos greeted us immediately. It was pitch black, and the only instructions we received were simple yet unnerving: **"RUN STRAIGHT UNTIL YOU HIT A WALL!"** Disoriented and burdened with gear, we scrambled into the darkness, the roar of the Chinook's blades fading behind us. When daylight broke, the precarious nature of our situation became clear. COP Michigan was a bowl-like depression surrounded by steep ridges, giving the enemy a perfect vantage point. Every movement felt exposed, a reminder that we were deep in enemy territory.

Life at COP Michigan was an unpredictable mix of monotony, chaos, and constant vigilance. Days blurred into weeks, marked by the ever-present threat of attack. My first firefight. The next morning was a baptism by fire. The chaos of combat—the deafening gunfire, the adrenaline surge, the surreal reality of being under attack—was overwhelming. Training kicked in, guiding my actions as my mind

29

struggled to catch up. Every patrol, checkpoint, and firefight felt like a battle for survival. The line between life and death blurred as days turned into weeks and weeks into months. At first, every burst of gunfire or distant mortar strike sent us scrambling to our positions, hearts pounding and adrenaline surging. Over time, exhaustion dulled those reactions. We learned to adapt, sometimes staying in bed for a few extra moments when the gunfire sounded less immediate. Yet, silence was never comforting. It wasn't peace; it was a warning—the enemy was planning, watching, and waiting for the perfect moment to strike.

Rocket-propelled grenades, mortar fire, and ambushes became a daily routine, each attack testing our endurance and courage. In those moments, the bond between us grew stronger. Together, we faced the chaos, leaned on each other for strength, and trusted one another with our lives.

There was a time where we were at our Observation Post (Pride Rock) on top of this mountain. Just the seven of us young soldiers facing the Korengal Valley for a week at a time. We had this tarp covering us tied by a four-inch cord to a sandbag to shield us from the summer sun. We soon started taking some small arms fire from something like Ak-74's and or other weapons. When bullets come towards you, you can tell how close it is based on if it wizzes, it's somewhat close, if it snaps, it's really close. Well, during this time I peaked my head out from behind the sandbags that were shielding me to try to see where the fire was coming from. The next thing that happened, I felt like someone just smacked my helmet. I remember stumbling, then falling on my back. I was dazed, and my ears were ringing, but I was confused because I didn't know what happened. My brother was next to me in this position and he saw me with a look of shock, thinking I had just been shot. He yelled **"ESPINOZA, ESPINOZA, ESPINOZA, ARE YOU GOOD?"**. I looked at him and yelled, **"I'M GOOD, I'M OK."** I looked up for some reason and saw the tarp flying and the cord was cut. A bullet cut the cord, which was one inch away from my helmet. That's what I felt.

Violence and death are realities of war, but in that comes a sense of peace. You come to terms that if it's your time to go, it's your time. There was a time where we were in an intense firefight. The odds were stacked against us, and I felt a sense that this was my time to go. I didn't feel sad for myself, but I felt sad for my family. I felt sad because my sisters back home were about to lose their brother, and my parents were going to lose their only son. I felt sad because my dad would take it the hardest. I know he was worried and scared for me being over here, but proud of his son. I just prayed that they have the strength to get through this. So I told myself, **"IF THIS IS MY TIME, THAT'S FINE BUT I'M GOING TO TAKE AS MANY AS OF THESE MOTHERFUCKERS WITH ME!"**

Life during this time was unrelenting. One moment you're eating food during dinner and the next moment you're running to help the incoming patrol after they have been attacked. You witness a friend and brother that you would crack jokes, seeing him with a hole in his chest from a rocket-propelled grenade, and his face is something you would never forget. It's walking to another position when an explosion knocks you back and you can't hear anything. You're thrown back on the ground on your back, thinking about what just happened. The dirt fills the air and you try to gather every inch of your being to get out of that area to somewhere that has cover.

31

▌ MISSIONS TO REMEMBER

Some missions blur into the background, but others remain etched in memory. One in particular stands out: a mission to escort a chaplain to another base. It should have been straightforward, but it quickly turned into a nightmare.

As the lead driver in our convoy, I carried immense responsibility and equal risk. Navigating a narrow dirt road through a small village, the first explosion hit. The blast rocked our vehicle, disorienting us as shrapnel tore through the air. Before we could process what had happened, a second explosion erupted, hitting the other side of our vehicle. RPGs and gunfire rained down from the ridges above.

Amid the chaos, my team leader's firm grip on my shoulder and steady voice broke through the noise: "**Drive!**" Somehow, I found the strength to push our disabled vehicle forward, navigating through the kill zone. This engagement was severe and intense, but through it all, it shows that no matter the odds against you have to fight. Not just for yourself, but for the people you serve with. That mission taught me something no training could: the instinct to act in the face of overwhelming fear and the unshakable trust in my team.

There was a mission we had to perform, which was a cordon and search of this particular village. Our intel stated they were enemy fighters, caches of weapons and explosives in this village, and our goal was to get rid of it. So this mission we left at dark and marched miles until we reached the village right before the morning sun showed itself. I was a machine gunner at the time, barely 140 pounds soaking wet, and carrying about 90 pounds of gear and ammo. When we arrived, we started doing what we trained for, what we were known for, searching rooms using violence of action. Anything that was there was searched, and we found what we needed.

Hours passed, and we finished our mission. Entering villages was the easy part, leaving the village is different. We knew if we didn't receive any gunfire when we entered, we sure as hell would receive it when we were leaving, and this time proved just that. As we were leaving our different positions in the village, we started receiving gunfire from the surrounding mountains. We returned fire, but during this time one of our squad leaders was hit multiple times which he needed to be flown out by a helicopter because he wouldn't live if he didn't get medical aid soon.

So, in order to provide more support for the helicopter to arrive, my squad was placed in a position to provide fire support. We had to climb this mountain about 600 yards of rock climbing, loose rocks to get to the area with the best possible support. Half way up this mountain my squad leader asked me "**Are you good?**" and I told him "**Yeah I'm good** ". But in my mind I said "**What the fuck you think? I'm exhausted carrying all this gear and ammo and your way bigger than me and you're seriously going to ask me that!**" So we got to our position and provided cover with our close air support, dropping bombs on the mountains. Big bombs that screamed "**AMERICA**".

The squad leader that was shot was flown out to a medical hospital, and we started closing our positions to leave the village. We started marching back to our base when our air support told us, "**We don't have enough fuel and we have to turn back. You're on your own** ". As soon as the air support left, we knew we had to pick up the pace and start running because the enemy knew that our air support was gone. Sure as shit, we were right. We started receiving fire, not a lot, but enough for us to pick up our pace for sure. Dead exhausted, you start doing anything in your power to feel lighter, and for me, it was throwing away the remaining ammo I had just to become that much faster. When you become that exhausted, you throw up while you're running, because you don't have the luxury to stop. We finally arrived at our base and a lot of us just looked at each other in a state of shock, but were also glad we made it back.

▮ THE BONDS FORGED IN FIRE

In the chaos of war, the bonds between soldiers became unbreakable. We weren't just comrades; we were brothers. We shared everything—our fears, our hopes, our victories, and our losses. One of my closest friends was a soldier named Carter. His humor and quick wit lightened even the darkest moments. During one particularly intense firefight, Carter's crazy comment — "**I DIDN'T SIGN UP FOR THIS SHIT!**"—brought a moment of levity that made us laugh despite the chaos.

But war is cruel. At this time, you come to sense that not everyone you're fighting with will go home. You become detached, sometimes not trying to know about their families back home, because if they don't make it home, you would think about their families. You think how hard they are going to take this news, that their son, brother, uncle or dad didn't make it. You become relentless, running to a position with bullets kicking dirt at your feet just to make it be there with your brother, or laughing when you're getting attacked. You try to forget anything at the time that clouds your judgement.

34

But you can sense how violence can impact the soul, you can see it in each other's eyes.

LESSONS LEARNED

Afghanistan taught me lessons I couldn't have learned anywhere else. I discovered the strength of perseverance, the value of discipline, and the importance of teamwork. But most profoundly, I learned the meaning of sacrifice.

The sacrifices we made—time away from family, the loss of friends, the toll on our bodies and minds—were immense. Yet we bore them willingly, driven by a sense of duty and loyalty.

Even now, those lessons remain with me. They shaped the man I am today, reminding me that no matter how difficult life becomes, there is always a way forward. After seeing the worst humans can do, you sense the beauty of a good thing and good people.

REFLECTIVE PAUSE

- **What sacrifices have you made in your life, and how have they shaped you?**
- **What lessons have you learned from the challenges you've faced?**
- **How do you honor the memory of those who have shaped your journey?**

These moments in Afghanistan changed me forever. They taught me that resilience isn't just about enduring—it's about growing stronger, and trying even when the odds seem against you. They reminded me that the bonds we form in hardship carry us through even the darkest days. And they proved that, even in chaos, there is purpose.

THE PSYCHOLOGICAL TOLL: A HEAVY BURDEN TO BEAR

War hardens you, but it also leaves scars—some visible, others buried deep in the recesses of your mind. My year in Afghanistan was a paradox: both the best and worst experience of my life. It forged me into a stronger, more resilient version of myself, but the cost was one I couldn't fully comprehend at the time.

I lost friends—brothers who fought beside me, shared meals with me, and laughed with me during fleeting moments of levity. Their deaths created a void no words could ever fill. The sounds of war—explosions, gunfire, the cries of the wounded—became an indelible backdrop to my life.

Grief, fear, and anger were emotions I tried to bury, telling myself I'd deal with them later. But war doesn't let you forget. It follows you. It lingers in your dreams, in quiet moments, and in the laughter of others—a stark reminder of what you've lost.

In the chaos of war, soldiers forge bonds that become unbreakable. We weren't just comrades—we were family. Connected by the shared reality of surviving a world few could imagine, we shared our fears, frustrations, and moments of triumph.

Coming home didn't bring the relief I'd hoped for. At just 19 years old, I carried the compounded weight of losing friends in combat and the devastating loss of my mother. The double blow left me hollow and directionless. Like many soldiers, I turned to alcohol as a crutch. The numbness it provided was temporary, offering a fleeting escape from the demons I was unwilling to face. But eventually I faced those demons head on and I was not going to be a victim.

I thought coming back home was supposed to feel like a relief. After the chaos and unpredictability of war, I thought stepping onto familiar soil would bring peace—a calm after the storm, a chance to finally exhale. Instead, it felt like stepping into a world I no longer recognized—a world that had moved on without me. The world I'd fought to protect felt foreign and disconnected from the one I'd lived in. Everyday activities like grocery shopping or family gatherings felt surreal. Fireworks on the Fourth of July didn't inspire celebration—they triggered vivid memories of mortar fire.

The silence was the first thing I noticed. It was deafening in its own way. After months of explosions, gunfire, and shouted commands, the stillness felt unnatural, even hostile. At first, it was a comfort. I slept soundly for the first time in months, unencumbered by the weight of my gear or the constant fear of attack. But as the days wore on, the silence became suffocating. It wasn't just the absence of noise; it was a reminder of all I had left behind—and all I would never truly leave behind.

Memories came in waves. Sometimes they were small and manageable; other times, they were overwhelming. A sound, a smell, or a sudden movement could send me back. I'd be standing in line at the grocery store, and suddenly I'd feel the weight of my rifle in my hands or hear the distant thud of mortars. I tried to bury these memories deep, but pain doesn't work that way. It demands to be felt.

In those early days, I struggled to cope. I turned to alcohol as a way to numb the pain. I wasn't drinking to get drunk; I drank just enough to dull the sharp edges of memories I wasn't ready to face. It was a temporary escape, a fleeting moment of quiet amid the chaos in my mind.

One of the hardest adjustments was feeling detached from those who hadn't shared my experience. I couldn't bridge the gap between their reality and mine. Conversations about trivial topics felt meaningless, and I found myself retreating into isolation, unable to imagine the burden I carried. I avoided people—not because I didn't love them, but because I didn't want them to see how much I was hurting. I told myself it was to protect them, to shield them from my pain. But isolation comes with its own cost. The more I pulled away, the harder it became to reconnect. I felt like a stranger in my own life, watching from a distance as the world moved on without me. Through it all, I discovered the true meaning of resilience. It isn't about pretending the pain doesn't exist; it's about finding the courage to face it, to let it shape you without letting it break you. Afghanistan didn't just test my endurance—it redefined it.

I stood at a crossroads: let the pain consume me or confront it. But confronting the pain wasn't as simple as flipping a switch. The weight of loss, the vivid memories of combat, and the guilt of surviving when others didn't was overwhelming. I knew if I didn't face my demons, they would consume me. Through it all, I discovered the true meaning of resilience. It isn't about pretending the pain doesn't exist; it's about finding the courage to face it, to let it shape you without letting it break you. Afghanistan didn't just test my endurance—it redefined it.

The experiences I endured there don't define me, but they've become an integral part of who I am. They are the foundation of a life built on purpose, determination, and strength. Resilience, I've learned, is the ability to take life's blows and stand back up—not because it's easy, but because giving up isn't an option.

War takes more than it gives. It strips away innocence, tests your limits, and forces you to confront truths about yourself and the world that you'd rather avoid. The cost of war for me was measured in the lives of friends lost, the haunting memories of battle, and the emotional toll that no amount of training could prepare me for.

Yet war also offered an invaluable perspective. It taught me to value life, to cherish peace, and to see beauty in moments of connection. The scars I carry, both visible and invisible, are reminders of the battles I've fought—and survived.

The lessons I learned in Afghanistan continue to shape my life. Discipline, teamwork, and the ability to push through fear are no longer just ideals—they're tools I use every day. I've come to see trauma not as a mark of weakness, but as an opportunity for growth. The scars I carry are badges of resilience, testaments to the strength that lies within all of us.

The friends I lost in Afghanistan are never far from my thoughts. I honor them by living a life that reflects the lessons they taught me: courage, loyalty, and the ability to find light, even in the darkest moments. Their sacrifices are a constant reminder to never take life for granted and to live with purpose and intention.

▌REFLECTIVE PAUSE

- What challenges in your life have shaped you into the person you are today?
- How have you found strength in the face of fear, loss, or uncertainty?
- What lessons can you take from the scars—both visible and invisible—that you carry?

In the end, it's not the pain that defines us, but how we choose to grow from it. The psychological toll of war is immense, but it also reveals the depth of human resilience and the capacity for growth in even the most trying circumstances.

CHAPTER 3

Marriage and "Normalcy"

In the midst of this turmoil, I made a decision that I hoped would anchor me: I got married. I was young and impulsive, and at the time, marriage seemed like the logical next step. I wanted what everyone else seemed to have—a family, stability, a "normal" life. It felt like the thing I had been fighting for, the reward waiting for me at the end of the battlefield.

But transitioning from the high-intensity world of deployment to the quiet monotony of civilian life was like stepping into a foreign land. The rules were different, the expectations unclear. In the military, my identity was tied to my mission, my purpose as part of something bigger than myself. Back home, that sense of purpose was gone.

I left the military and tried to find my footing in the civilian world. I took on jobs that felt mundane compared to the life-or-death stakes I had grown accustomed to. Every day felt like a grind, but not the kind of grind that built resilience or camaraderie. It was the kind of grind that wore you down that left you questioning your place in the world.

No one tells you how hard it is to find purpose after you've had a mission so deeply ingrained in you. In the military, I knew exactly who I was and what I was fighting for. Back home, I felt like a stranger in my own life. I couldn't share my experiences with family or friends because they couldn't relate—and, frankly, I didn't want to scare them.

War changes you in ways that are hard to put into words. War impacts your life knowing the destruction you're capable of, but you restrain yourself to show your true strength. It sharpens your instincts, heightens your senses, and leaves you with a constant awareness of your surroundings. But it also leaves scars—emotional ones that are invisible to the naked eye but deeply felt. I had seen things, done things that I couldn't put into words. And even if I could, I wasn't sure I wanted anyone else to carry that weight with me.

My marriage became another battleground—not of bullets and explosions, but of unspoken pain and unmet expectations. I wanted to provide for my family, to be the husband and father I thought I was supposed to be. But how do you show up fully for others when you're still trying to piece yourself back together?

I tried to find balance, but it always felt just out of reach. I poured myself into work, thinking that if I could just provide enough— money, stability, security—it would make up for the things I couldn't give emotionally. But love doesn't work that way. You can't build a strong foundation on material things alone.

Looking back, I see now that I was chasing an idea of normalcy that didn't exist. I thought that if I followed the script—get a job, get married, start a family—it would somehow make everything fall into place. But life isn't a script, and normalcy is an illusion.

The hardest part was realizing that no amount of effort could make up for the cracks in the foundation. My marriage began to falter under the weight of unspoken pain and unmet needs. I wanted to be everything for my family, but I didn't know how to be that person when I was still grappling with my own sense of identity.

Returning home wasn't the relief I had hoped for, but it was a turning point. It forced me to confront the parts of myself I had been running from, to acknowledge the pain I had tried to bury. It wasn't an easy process—it's still not—but it was necessary.

I've learned that healing doesn't happen all at once. It's a slow, often painful process of peeling back layers and facing what lies beneath. It's about learning to live with the scars, to let them remind you not just of what you've been through, but of what you've survived.

The silence that once felt suffocating has become a space for reflection. The vices I once leaned on no longer hold the same power over me. And the relationships I once withdrew from have become lifelines, reminders that I'm not alone in this journey.

▌REFLECTIVE PAUSE:

- **What moments in your life have forced you to confront the parts of yourself you've been avoiding?**
- **How have you found strength in the process of rebuilding?**

The road back to me has been anything but smooth, but it's a road I'm grateful to be on. Coming home wasn't the end of my story—it was the beginning of a new chapter, one that I'm still learning how to write. And while the "unknown" still looms large, I've come to see it not as something to fear, but as something to embrace.

THE ROLE OF THE PROVIDER

The lessons I learned during my first deployment extended far beyond the battlefield—they shaped how I approached every aspect of my life. In relationships, I adopted a "no quit" mentality. I believed with all my heart that if both people put in the effort, anything could be fixed. To me, love and commitment meant resilience, perseverance, and never giving up. But life has a way of teaching us hard truths, and one of the most difficult lessons I had to learn was that effort alone isn't enough to save a relationship if it's one-sided.

I wanted to be the provider I thought I was supposed to be—the man who worked tirelessly to ensure his family had everything they needed. Growing up, I hadn't had the best role models when it came to healthy relationships. I watched more dysfunction than connection, more arguments than affection. But there was one lesson I held onto tightly: a man provides. I thought that if I worked hard, paid the bills, and kept a roof over our heads, I'd be doing my part.

What I didn't realize at the time was that providing on a surface level isn't enough. True provision goes beyond material things; it's about being emotionally present, building trust, and nurturing a connection that withstands life's inevitable storms. Without that emotional connection, even the strongest foundation can crumble.

In hindsight, I can see where I went wrong. I worked so hard to fulfill what I thought were my duties as a provider that I overlooked the emotional gaps forming in my marriage. I thought love could be measured in hours worked, in sacrifices made, in bills paid. But love isn't a transaction—it's an investment. It requires attention, patience, and vulnerability. And I wasn't giving enough of those things.

If there's one role I've tried to get right above all others, it's being a father. When my daughter was born, something shifted inside me. She became my guiding light, the reason I pushed myself even when I felt like I had nothing left to give. I made a vow to give her a better childhood than the one I had—a childhood filled with love, stability, and opportunity.

Parenthood doesn't come with a manual. You figure it out as you go, stumbling and failing along the way. But for me, failure wasn't an option. I was determined to give my daughter everything I could, even if it meant sacrificing my own happiness. When she was little, I worked tirelessly to provide for her and my wife. I took on whatever jobs paid the bills, even if they weren't fulfilling or aligned with my passions.

There were times when I felt like I was doing everything right, but there was always that nagging voice in the back of my mind telling me I wasn't enough. Society places immense pressure on men to measure their worth by their ability to provide. And when you fall short—even for a moment—it can leave you questioning your value.

Looking back, I realize that the greatest gift I could give my daughter wasn't financial security or material things—it was my time, my presence, and my love. I wish I had understood that sooner.

LESSONS IN PROVISION

The role of the provider is often glorified, but rarely examined deeply. What does it really mean to provide? Is it about working long hours and sacrificing your own needs for others? Or is it about showing up in every sense—physically, emotionally, and mentally?

I'm still answering that question for myself, but I've learned a few things along the way. Providing isn't just about giving things; it's about giving yourself. It's about creating a safe, loving environment where your loved one's feel seen, heard, and valued. I thought I was doing the right thing by working so hard, but I lost sight of what truly mattered. My daughter didn't need me to buy her things; she needed me to be there. My wife didn't need me to work myself to the bone; she needed a partner to share life's joys and burdens.

The lessons from those years have I have tried to shape how I approach relationships and fatherhood today. True provision is about balance—between giving and receiving, working and resting, striving and simply being present.

REFLECTIVE PAUSE

- **What does it mean to truly provide for the people you love?**
- **How do we balance the demands of work and life without losing sight of what's most important?**

The role of the provider is a noble one, but it's also challenging. It requires not just strength and resilience, but also vulnerability and self-awareness. And perhaps the most important lesson of all: you can't pour from an empty cup. To truly provide for others, you must also take care of yourself.

A MISGUIDED DEFINITION OF SUCCESS

Looking back on my marriage, I see how much I underestimated the importance of emotional depth. I thought I was doing everything right—working tirelessly to provide, protecting my family, and giving them a stable life. But all of these efforts were surface-level. They lacked the emotional connection that makes a relationship truly strong.

When I got married, I believed I was following the script of life: grow up, get married, have kids, work hard, and eventually retire. I thought this was how success was measured. But life doesn't follow a script, and relationships don't come with instruction manuals. I learned that lesson the hard way.

I thought being a good husband and father meant ensuring my family's material needs were met. I worked long hours to pay the bills, fill the fridge, and keep a roof over our heads. But I didn't realize relationships require much more than financial stability. They need connection, intimacy, and shared vulnerability.

My daughter's birth brought an immediate shift in my priorities. She became my driving force, the reason I kept pushing forward despite the exhaustion. I worked every job I could find, often feeling like I was stuck in an endless cycle of providing without ever feeling like I was doing enough.

Society often ties a man's worth to his ability to provide, and I fell into that trap. When I felt I wasn't meeting those expectations, it cut deeply, leaving me questioning my value as a husband and father.

Even as I struggled to connect with my wife, I worked to be the best father I could. Parenting is a journey of trial and error, and I was determined to give my daughter the love and support I had longed for as a child.

I poured myself into providing for her, sacrificing time and energy in the process. But in hindsight, I realize that being a father isn't just about providing material security—it's about being present. The moments I missed can never be replaced, and I wish I had understood sooner how much those small, everyday moments mean in a child's life. In an attempt to provide more for my family.

▌ LEAVING AGAIN

Despite my best intentions, In an attempt to provide more for my family life pulled me back into the world I thought I had left behind. I took a job as a private contractor, deploying overseas again—this time to Afghanistan and Guantanamo Bay. The job took me to Afghanistan for three years, with a brief break halfway through. The decision wasn't an easy one, but it felt necessary. The work offered financial stability, and a renewed sense of purpose that I had been missing since leaving the military.

My daughter was about five when I left. She was too young to fully understand why I had gone or what I was doing. All she could comprehend was that her dad was far away, out of sight. My attempts to bridge that distance lay in frequent phone calls and video chats whenever and wherever possible. Yet, nothing replaces being physically present. I knew I was missing precious moments in her life—moments that could never be recaptured.

The work I undertook overseas was grueling, and confidentiality agreements bind me from revealing too much. However, I can say this much—it was both a blessing and a curse. On one hand, it filled a void in me, giving a renewed sense of purpose I had not felt in years. On the other, it took me away from my family at a time when they needed me most.

I stayed overseas for three years, with only a brief return midway through. By that point, the cracks in my marriage had become more apparent. I had always assured my wife, "**If it becomes too much for you, I'll come home**." But that call never came.

REBUILDING DREAMS, CONFRONTING REALITY

When I returned home for good in 2020, I was ready to rebuild my life. After years overseas, I envisioned a fresh start: reconnecting with my wife and daughter, and finally creating the stable, loving family life I had always dreamed of. But reality was far more complicated than I had imagined. Something had shifted in my absence. I found a home that felt unfamiliar, almost like a place I no longer belonged to—off-kilter in ways I couldn't quite describe. Absence and Its Strain the separation wasn't just measured in physical distance but emotional as well. Both of us developed a hollow inside that we didn't know how to fill. When I returned, I hoped life could resume as it had been before I left. But relationships don't work that way. Time had marched forward, altering us in ways neither of us could have foreseen. My Wife seemed detached, her mind preoccupied with thoughts she didn't share. I wanted to reconnect with her, to repair the widening gap between us. But our communication felt like trying to speak two different languages. Each passing day seemed to widen the emotional distance further. She seemed distant, as if a quiet wall had risen between us during the years I was away. The emotional connection that once bound us together felt frayed, if not completely severed. At first, I rationalized it. Maybe it was the adjustment period; after all, I'd been gone for so long. I told myself she just needed time to rediscover herself and reconnect with friends and family.

In my efforts to provide for my family, I had overlooked the true cost of my absence. Providing isn't just about paying bills; it's about presence—being there for the small, seemingly insignificant moments that stitch a family together. Bedtime stories, shared meals, and those silent, unspoken connections that form only when you're physically present. Those were the things I had neglected, and I hadn't realized how much they mattered—until they were gone.

But as time went on, her absences became harder to ignore. She started going out more often, leaving me at home with our daughter. Her excuses—visiting family, catching up with old friends—were vague, and the frequency of her outings gnawed at me. I couldn't shake the feeling that something was wrong. I chose to ignore the signs at first, burying my doubts under a facade of optimism. After all, I was finally home with my family—that should have been enough. I convinced myself the cracks in our relationship were temporary, something we could mend with time and effort. But deep down, I knew something fundamental had changed.

█ A GUT FEELING

Shortly after I came home, my wife became pregnant. My initial reaction was joy—why wouldn't I be happy? But deep down, something felt off, an unshakable instinct I couldn't explain.

At first, I ignored it, focusing instead on rebuilding my life with my family. But her absences became more frequent, her explanations more vague. She spent nights at a friend's house and returned the next day with stories that didn't add up.

The doubts gnawed at me, but I tried to rationalize them. I told myself she just needed time to readjust. Then I found a document suggesting she was weeks pregnant before I came home. When I confronted her, her explanation was unconvincing, and the cracks in our marriage turned into chasms.

One night, I saw her turn off the headlights before pulling into our driveway. It struck me as strange, but I chose to let it go. The next day, the weight of my suspicions became unbearable. When I confronted her directly about seeing someone else, she denied it. But the trust had already eroded. The unraveling of our marriage reached its breaking point. The life I had envisioned—the life I had worked so hard to provide—was gone.

The first major blow came when I discovered the financial security I thought I had built was gone. While I was overseas, I entrusted my wife with managing our finances, believing the money I worked so hard to earn—money I risked my life for—was being saved for our future.

But upon my return, I discovered bills had piled up, and our savings account was nearly empty. I felt blindsided and betrayed.

The financial stability I had sacrificed so much to provide had vanished, and I couldn't understand how it had happened. I replayed the choices I'd made, asking myself if I'd been naïve to trust her so completely. But the "why" didn't matter as much as the reality: I had come home to a situation that felt entirely out of my control.

THE BREAKING POINT

The breaking point came during a conversation I'll never forget. My wife suggested, almost casually, that I consider deploying again. It wasn't just the suggestion itself that hurt—it was the ease with which she said it, as if sending me back to a life that had already taken so much from me was the simplest solution.

For years, I had fought battles overseas, enduring physical and emotional scars for the sake of my family. To hear her so readily push me back into that life, without hesitation or concern for what it might cost me, was a wake-up call.

At that moment, I realized our marriage wasn't what I thought it was. The partnership we once shared had been replaced by something unrecognizable. And while I could accept the pain of losing a relationship, what hurt most was the impact it had on my daughter. She was the innocent bystander in all of this, caught in the crossfire of a marriage falling apart.

A MOMENT CLOUDED B Y DOUBT

The day the baby was born should have been a moment of joy—a milestone in our marriage, a celebration of new life. Instead, it was overshadowed by tension and doubt, a heaviness that filled the delivery room like an unspoken truth.

At the time, I was out of town, training for a new job. When my wife called to tell me she was in labor, my immediate response was, "I'm on my way." Her answer stopped me cold: "You don't have to come."

Those words stung, but I didn't let them deter me. Despite everything we had been through, I was still her husband. This was our family—or so I thought. I dropped everything and rushed to the hospital, determined to be there for the birth of the child I believed was mine.

When I arrived, her reaction was far from welcoming. She seemed upset by my presence, as though it was more of an inconvenience than a comfort. Even as I sat beside her, I felt the chasm between us—the emotional connection we once shared had vanished.

As the baby was born, I wanted to feel joy. I wanted to believe this was a fresh start for our family. But deep down, the nagging doubts I had been suppressing for months came rushing back. Something wasn't right, and the weight of that realization made it impossible to fully embrace the moment.

The months that followed widened the cracks in our marriage into an unbridgeable divide. The distance between us grew unbearable, and the strain seeped into every corner of our lives. Eventually, my wife made a decision that shattered me: she took our daughter and the newborn child and left without explanation.

For weeks, I had no idea where they were. My calls and texts went unanswered, and the silence was suffocating. The house felt hollow without my daughter's laughter and presence, a constant reminder of everything I was losing.

Desperate to see my daughter again, I reached out to my wife's parents. I demanded to know where she was, making it clear that I wouldn't stop until I found her. Those weeks of separation were some of the hardest of my life—a volatile mix of anger, sadness, and helplessness.

Eventually, I learned her location. With the help of my sisters and some painful digging, the truth began to emerge. I discovered that while I was overseas, my wife had been seeing someone else. The late-night absences, the vague excuses, the growing emotional distance—it all made sense.

The hardest blow came with the realization that the newborn child wasn't mine. Deep down, I think I already knew. But facing the truth head-on was devastating.

THE HARDEST CONVERSATION

The weight of betrayal and loss is one thing; seeing it reflected in your child's eyes is something else entirely. One of the most difficult conversations I've ever had was with my daughter. It wasn't planned, but the moment felt inevitable—a truth that could no longer be avoided. We were driving home one day, the hum of the engine filling the silence between us, when I looked at her through the rearview mirror and said, "**Mamas, I know what your mom has been doing.**" The shift in her demeanor was immediate.

Her eyes, filled with relief, glistened with unshed tears. It was as though a burden she had been carrying alone was suddenly lifted.

She began to speak, her small voice trembling as she recounted stories that no child should have to tell. She told me how her mom had asked her to lie to me, how she had been left alone in the house at just six years old for a couple of hours, and how that moment had scared her. The pain in her voice was tough to hear as a father, but what broke me was when she started to apologize. **"I'M SORRY, DAD"** she said, tears streaming down her face, as though any of it could have been her fault. I pulled the car over, turned around, and looked her in the eyes. **"It's okay,"** I told her firmly. **"You're a child. You don't need to be sorry"**. That moment solidified something for me: no matter what happens, I will always show up for my daughter. I couldn't protect her from everything—life had made that painfully clear—but I could make sure she never doubted how deeply she was loved. The guilt of not being able to shield her from all the pain she had endured will stay with me forever. But in that moment, I vowed to be her anchor, the steady presence she could always rely on.

STRENGTH IN RESTRAINT

The pain of betrayal brings with it a temptation—a temptation to lash out, to let anger dictate your actions. I know what I'm capable of; my time in the military in the chaos of war has shown me the depths of destruction I can unleash. But through all of this, I've come to understand that true strength isn't measured by how much damage you can cause—it's measured by how much you can endure without losing yourself.

There were moments in my life when my anger threatened to consume me. I'd think of the loss, lies, the neglect, and the betrayal, and it would feel like too much. I knew what I was capable of—I had seen that side of myself no one has seen. But I also knew that acting on anger would only add to the pain my daughter had already endured.

Strength isn't about how much damage you can do; it's about how much you can endure without breaking. My daughter didn't need a father who fought battles out of rage; she needed one who could stand tall, even in the face of anything life has to offer. Every choice I made was guided by her needs, her well-being, and her future.

Fatherhood is a relentless pursuit of love. It's about waking up every day and choosing to show up, no matter how difficult the circumstances are. My commitment to my daughter became the driving force behind every decision I made.

When I biked 10 miles each way to work, it wasn't for me—it was for her. Every mile was a promise that I would always do whatever it took to provide for her. The physical exhaustion paled in comparison to the joy of seeing her face light up when I came home.

Even my decision to take a contracting job overseas was rooted in my desire to secure her future. The money was good, and I believed it was the best way to provide for her long-term. But the chaos of war had its pull, too. It was a world I understood—a place where my actions had clear consequences. The quiet responsibilities of home, by contrast, felt foreign and overwhelming.

Looking back, I question whether the sacrifices I made were always the right ones. **Did my absence create gaps in her life that I can't ever fully fill? Did I trade precious moments for the illusion of stability?** These questions weigh heavily on me, but they also fuel my determination to make every moment count moving forward.

THE PATERNITY TEST

After uncovering the betrayal, I filed for divorce and requested a paternity test. My wife initially resisted, claiming it would harm the child's innocence. But I didn't care. I needed closure, and this was the only way to get it.

When the results came back, they confirmed what I already knew: the baby wasn't mine. Even though I had prepared myself, seeing it in black and white was like a punch to the gut. It was a moment of finality, both painful and clarifying.

Losing the family I thought I had—the future I had envisioned— was one of the hardest things I've ever endured. But in hindsight, it was for the best. The truth, as painful as it was, allowed me to begin the process of healing.

LESSONS IN LOSS

The betrayal and heartbreak forced me to reevaluate not just my marriage, but myself. It taught me lessons I never expected to learn.

Authenticity Matters: In my marriage, I often felt I had to change who I was to fit a mold. I dressed, spoke, and acted in ways that didn't feel true to myself. I now understand that healthy

57

relationships require authenticity—not just with your partner, but with yourself. A strong foundation can't be built on pretense.

Forgiveness: Forgiveness was one of the hardest lessons to learn. It wasn't just about forgiving my ex-wife for the betrayal—it was about forgiving myself for the mistakes I made, the signs I ignored, and the choices that led me to that point. Forgiveness doesn't excuse the hurt; it releases you from its grip.

Resilience is Key: The experience taught me that resilience isn't just about surviving—it's about learning, growing, and emerging stronger. Betrayal cuts deep, but it doesn't define you. How you choose to move forward does.

The end of my marriage forced me to confront difficult truths about myself and my understanding of relationships. I had focused so much on being a provider that I neglected the emotional connections that make a family strong.

I realized that provision isn't just about material stability—it's about emotional presence, trust, and vulnerability. Relationships can't thrive when one partner is carrying all the weight, and communication is the bridge that keeps bonds intact.

Letting go of my marriage wasn't about giving up; it was about recognizing that I couldn't fix something alone. Some battles require both partners to fight, and sometimes the healthiest choice is to walk away. Letting go felt like admitting defeat—a concept that didn't sit well with my "NO QUIT" mentality. But sometimes, the strongest thing you can do is release what's no longer serving you.

I wrestled with guilt and uncertainty. **Had I done enough? Could I have fought harder**? These questions haunted me, but deep down, I knew the truth: I couldn't save something that required both of us to fight. I couldn't pour from an empty cup.

Despite everything, I've come to respect the man my ex-wife is now with. He treats my daughter well, and for that, I'm grateful. We're not friends, and we probably never will be, but I can acknowledge his role in her life. Sometimes life doesn't give us the outcomes we hope for, but we have a choice in how we respond.

The unraveling of my marriage marked the end of one chapter and the beginning of another. It forced me to confront my deepest fears, reevaluate my priorities, and redefine what I wanted out of life and relationships.

I approach relationships differently now. I no longer seek perfection or try to fit into societal molds. Instead, I value authenticity, emotional depth, and mutual respect. Love isn't about meeting expectations—it's about building something real.

Most importantly, I've learned to value myself. My worth isn't defined by someone else's actions or decisions. It's defined by how I choose to move forward, by the lessons I carry with me, and by the life I build for myself and my daughter.

▌ REFLECTIVE PAUSE

- **What heartbreaks have shaped you, and what lessons did they teach?**
- **How have those experiences influenced the way you approach life and relationships today?**

For me, the betrayal and loss were painful, but they also became a turning point. They taught me to embrace authenticity, seek deeper connections, and value my own worth. And while the journey hasn't been easy, it has been one of growth, resilience, and rediscovery. Every scar tells a story, and every story is a testament to how far we've come.

▌ MOVING FORWARD AS A FATHER

While my marriage ended, my role as a father always was my focus. My daughter remained my anchor, the reason I continued to push forward. I made a conscious effort to be more present in her life, to show her that even though her parents' marriage didn't survive, she was deeply loved and valued.

Being a father isn't about perfection—it's about showing up, even when life feels overwhelming. It's about being vulnerable enough to admit when you've made mistakes and determined enough to do better.

If there's one role I've tried to get right above all others, it's being a father. When my daughter was born, something shifted inside me. She became my guiding light, the reason I pushed myself even when I felt like I had nothing left to give. I made a vow to give her a better childhood than the one I had—a childhood filled with love, stability, and opportunity.

Parenthood doesn't come with a manual. You stumble, fail, and figure it out as you go. For me, failure wasn't an option. I was determined to give my daughter everything I could, even if it meant sacrificing my own happiness. I took on any job that paid the bills, no matter how unfulfilling, because I wanted to provide for her and my wife.

But there were times when I felt like I wasn't enough. Society places immense pressure on men to measure their worth by their ability to provide. And when you fall short, even briefly, it can leave you questioning your value. Looking back now, I realize the greatest gift I could give my daughter wasn't financial security or material things—it was my time, my presence, and my love. I wish I had understood that sooner.

When my relationship with my daughter's mother ended, I found myself in uncharted territory. Being a single father was a role I hadn't anticipated, and there was no map to guide me. I leaned on my sisters for advice, scoured the internet late at night for answers, and embraced the messy, trial-and-error nature of parenting.

One of the most humbling experiences came when my daughter was too scared to sleep alone. Night after night, I laid a blanket on the floor next to her bed, sacrificing my own comfort to ensure her sense of safety. Those sleepless nights were a reminder that fatherhood isn't about grand gestures—it's about showing up, again and again, in the small, quiet moments that matter most.

When Lola entered our lives later on, things began to shift. Her presence brought a sense of calm and security that helped my daughter find the courage to sleep in her own room. For the first time in months, I wasn't sleeping on the floor. Watching my daughter grow more comfortable in Lola's presence was a gift—a testament to the power of love and the importance of the people we bring into our children's lives.

Fatherhood isn't about having all the answers. It's about doing whatever it takes to ensure your child feels loved, supported, and safe. Whether it's riding a bike to work, making sacrifices to provide financial stability, or simply holding their hand during the hardest conversations, every act of love builds the foundation they'll stand on for the rest of their lives.

For me, that foundation is still a work in progress. I've made mistakes, and I've had to face hard truths about myself and my choices. But through it all, my promise to my daughter remains unbroken: I will always show up for her. I will always fight for her. And I will always love her unconditionally.

▌ REFLECTIVE PAUSE

- **What does redemption look like in your life?**
- **How do you reconcile the sacrifices you've made with the lessons you've learned along the way?**

For me, redemption isn't about erasing the past—it's about learning from it. It's about becoming the father my daughter needs, not despite my mistakes, but because of them. It's about persistence, resilience, and the unwavering commitment to love her with everything I have.

Fatherhood isn't about perfection; it's about presence. It's about showing up, day after day, and letting your love speak louder than your shortcomings. And in that, I've found a deeper understanding of what it means to truly be a father.

Looking back, I don't see my marriage as a failure—it was a lesson. It taught me the importance of emotional depth, the dangers of neglecting connection, and the value of being present. These lessons, though painful, have shaped me into a better father and a more self-aware person.

Moving forward, I carry those lessons with me, determined not to repeat the mistakes of the past. I strive to build relationships that are grounded in trust, mutual support, and vulnerability. Most importantly, I aim to be the father my daughter deserves—a constant presence in her life, someone she can always rely on for love, guidance, and support.

THE STRUGGLE OF CO-PARENTING: BUILDING A LEGACY OF LOVE

Co-parenting was never a challenge I expected to face, but life rarely unfolds as planned. When my marriage ended, I didn't just lose a partner—I gained a new role that required navigating uncharted emotional terrain with someone I trusted at one point in time. What remained constant was our daughter, a living embodiment of our shared history and our shared responsibility. She deserved our best, even when giving it felt nearly impossible.

The early days of co-parenting were some of the hardest. Every interaction with my daughter's mother felt like walking through a minefield of unspoken pain and resentment. Custody exchanges were fraught with tension, often punctuated by the kind of silence that says more than words ever could. The presence of new men in her life reopened wounds I thought I had begun to heal. It felt as if I was caught between fighting to protect my daughter and trying to process my own heartbreak.

One of the defining moments of my co-parenting journey came when I had to confront both my daughter's mother and her then-partner. It wasn't easy to sit across from them and lay out my boundaries—to state firmly what was and wasn't acceptable when it came to our daughter. But I realized that this wasn't about power or control; it was about love and responsibility.

At that moment, I chose my daughter over my ego. I chose to prioritize her safety, stability, and happiness over my anger. Letting go of resentment wasn't about absolving anyone of blame—it was about freeing myself from the weight of emotions that no longer served me. I couldn't change what had happened, but I could choose how I showed up moving forward. Through Lola's mother guidance, she helped me see it that way.

Restraint became my quiet superpower. I knew what I was capable of—years in the military. The acts of violence I've committed had taught me how to channel my anger. But being a father required a different kind of strength. It meant holding back, even when every fiber of my being wanted to unleash the hurt I felt. Strength wasn't about reacting to the pain; it was about rising above it.

Parenting isn't just about compromise—it's about persistence. It's about showing up for the small, everyday moments and not just the big milestones. One of the most humbling parts of my journey was the time I spent sleeping on the floor of my daughter's room because she was too afraid to sleep alone. Night after night, I laid down next to her bed, the carpet floor becoming a silent witness to my determination to make her feel safe.

Those moments were exhausting, but they were also a reminder of what fatherhood is truly about. It's not about grand gestures or flashy displays of love—it's about the quiet, consistent acts of care that build trust over time. It's about being the person your child can rely on, no matter what.

▌ FATHERHOOD

Fatherhood has taught me patience, resilience, and the importance of showing up, even when it's hard. It's taught me that love isn't just a feeling—it's a choice you make every day. It's in the sacrifices, the compromises, and the moments when you feel like you're failing but refuse to give up.

Parenting without a map has been the hardest journey of my life, but it's also been the most rewarding. My daughter has been my greatest teacher, showing me the power of unconditional love and the strength of vulnerability. Every time she looks at me with trust in her eyes, I'm reminded that the struggles are worth it.

My daughter has showed me that the world is not as cruel as some people tend to see. She has opened my eyes to see the beautiful things in life. There are times she would draw pictures next to me and ask me how they were. She's a kid learning, but I could see the look in her eyes where she wants my honest opinion. She taught me that being a dad isn't about being tough all the times but allowing yourself to show a gentle side to yourself. She would try to put my hair in different hair styles but I see could hear laughing and the smile on her face made it worth it.

When my daughter looks back on her childhood, I hope she remembers more than the moments I got wrong. I hope she sees the nights I slept on the floor beside her, the miles I rode to get to work, and the times I cheered the loudest at her school recitals. I hope she remembers a father who never stopped trying, who loved her fiercely, and who showed up every single day. While I wasn't perfect, I did whatever I could to be there for her to give her a good life, showing her the love she deserves.

Legacy isn't about perfection; it's about presence. It's about the love you pour into the everyday moments—the bedtime stories, the walks to the park, the shared laughter over inside jokes. It's about being there, even when it's hard, even when you're tired, even when you're unsure.

▌ REFLECTIVE PAUSE

- **What kind of legacy do you hope to leave for your children?**
- **How do you want them to remember you, not just as a parent, but as a person?**

For me, the answer is simple: I want my daughter to know that she was, and always will be, my greatest priority. I want her to remember a father who loved her unconditionally, who made mistakes but never stopped trying, and who always showed up for her, no matter what.

Because at the end of the day, fatherhood isn't about being perfect—it's about being present. It's about loving your child so deeply that you're willing to do whatever it takes to make their world brighter, safer, and filled with possibility. If my daughter carries that with her, then I'll know I've done something right.

CHAPTER 4

Lola: A Shooting Star

Meeting Lola felt like stepping into a story where you already know the ending will matter. It wasn't just an encounter; it was an awakening. Her eyes met mine, and it wasn't simply a glance—it was a conversation, an unspoken understanding that transcended words. I felt, in that instant, that a force greater than chance had arranged our meeting. She was a beautiful, spicy personality, with curly black hair I would never forget. She didn't dress up and was in casual clothes, which made our meeting evening better and I loved how she was just herself.

That evening, I visited her house with no expectations. She had a dog that had a shock collar on, just in case. I thought the dog was going to attack me from the beginning, but the dog loved me for some reason. Since some believe animals judge character well, I must have passed their test; I certainly wasn't complaining about not being attacked. What started as a polite introduction quickly became hours of conversation. The conversations felt effortless. Even the silences carried a weight of comfort rather than awkwardness. It was as though the world had briefly stopped spinning, allowing us to exist in a bubble of connection that only we could access.

With Lola, I experienced a rare kind of ease. She embraced my quirks rather than tolerating them. My corny jokes didn't just earn polite chuckles; they were met with her genuine laughter and equally playful shit talking. It felt like we were composing a melody only the two of us could hear, one that grew richer with every exchange.

Was it fate, serendipity, or something more profound? I still wrestle with those questions. But one thing remains clear: meeting Lola was a pivotal moment, one that reshaped the course of my life.

From the beginning, being with Lola felt unlike anything I'd experienced before. This wasn't just about chemistry or attraction— though both were undeniably present. It was about a connection so deep it felt like she could see through the layers I had built to protect myself.

After my divorce, I had promised myself I would approach my next relationship with openness. With Lola, keeping that promise felt effortless. For the first time, I felt truly seen—not for what I could provide, but for who I was. Lola had a way of looking at me that made me feel enough, as though I didn't have to prove or perform to earn her love. That realization was as liberating as it was terrifying.

Lola wasn't someone who wore her heart on her sleeve, but when she let me glimpse her vulnerability, it felt like a gift. Her fierce independence often clashed with my instinct to protect, yet it was part of what made her so interesting. She didn't need saving; she needed partnership.

After a few months together, I made the decision to introduce Lola to my daughter—a choice I did not take lightly. Bringing someone new into her life after my divorce wasn't something I approached casually. But with Lola, it felt right.

The introduction was nothing short of magical. My daughter, typically shy and slow to trust, gravitated to Lola almost immediately. There was an ease in their interaction, a natural bond that seemed to form without effort. My daughter would light up when Lola was around, her laughter filling the spaces that had felt quiet and heavy for too long.

When Lola came into our lives, everything began to shift. For the first time in months, my daughter felt safe enough to sleep in her own bed. It was a small victory, but one that spoke volumes about the impact Lola had on both of us. Watching my daughter open up to her reminded me of the importance of the people we bring into our children's lives.

Watching them together was transformative. Seeing my daughter connect with someone I loved deepened my feelings for Lola in ways I hadn't anticipated. It wasn't just about my love for her; it was about the joy and comfort she brought to my daughter's life. They were inseparable together, always laughing. They would dance and I see my daughter be truly herself, letting her wild side show. Both of them loved making fun of me or teasing me, which just seeing them smile and laugh made it ok.

When my daughter was with Lola, she was Lola's mini me. She always wanted to do the things Lola did. When Lola curled her hair, my daughter mysteriously wanted to curl her hair, when Lola blow dried her hair, my daughter would want to blow dry her hair. I remember there were times when I could see my daughter looking at Lola, smiling without Lola noticing. Lola had no idea the impact she was on this little girl, looking at Lola as a role model. Any time I would tell my daughter I was going to see Lola when my daughter was not with me, she would get upset saying "**I WANT TO GO**". When my daughter was with me, she would always ask if we were going to Lola's or if she was coming over with a smile on her face. My daughter would have pictures of all three of us together on her wall and sometimes it would help her sleep at night.

▌ NO LOVE WITHOUT STRUGGLES

No love story is without its struggles, and ours was no exception. From the moment I met Lola, I knew her life was shadowed by battles she didn't openly share. Her past had left scars—hidden yet ever-present. Those scars shaped the way she loved, trusted, and protected herself. She was guarded, cautious, hesitant to fully let down her walls. I understood it, even respected it, but that understanding didn't make things easier.

I wanted to give her a love so steadfast it could stand against any storm. I wanted to show her that no matter how hard things got, I wouldn't fall. But love, I've learned, isn't one person carrying the weight alone—it's a partnership. And while I tried to meet her where she was, I wasn't without my own flaws. But through it all, even knowing the obstacles, I still tried because I cared deeply, loved her that much, and she was worth it to my daughter and me.

In my eagerness to make her happy, I often stepped back, letting her take the lead. At the time, I thought I was being supportive—giving her the space to feel comfortable, secure, and in control. But looking back, I see how I might have seemed passive or detached. Love, I learned too late, requires balance. It's a dance between giving and leading, between compromise and standing firm.

There's a fine line between caring deeply and the other, seeing that showing the same effort too. I hadn't considered that balance before Lola. I didn't realize that always deferring to her could send the wrong message—not one of care, but of disengagement or assertiveness. Only after losing her did I begin to deeply reflect on my actions and see how I could have better balanced our relationship.

▌ MOMENTS OF VULNERABILITY

Defining moments in a relationship often comes unexpectedly, and with Lola, one stands out vividly. One morning, she called me, her voice strained with fear. She was heading to the ER with chest pain. Without hesitation, I told her, **"I'm on my way."**

I left work early, got in my car, and drove hours to be with her. When I arrived, the cold wrapped around me like a harsh reminder of my helplessness. They didn't allow me inside because of strict COVID protocols. Lola, ever selfless, told me to go to her home and rest, assuring me that she would be alright. But I couldn't leave her. My place was there, as close to her as the situation allowed.

I sat on a cold bench outside the hospital, watching her through the glass window of the waiting area. She sat alone, unaware of my gaze. I silently willed her to be okay. When she was admitted, I told the staff, "**THAT'S MY WIFE**," even though we weren't married. It didn't matter to me. At that moment, she was my world. She was shocked when I arrived in her room because she didn't expect me to get inside the hospital. In my mind, I told myself, "**I'm getting in that room no matter what, either they let me in or I'm sneaky in, but regardless I'm getting in**". During this time, I remember she cried and didn't want me to see. She has a strong will personality to her so when she cried i just hugged her and told her "**It's Ok**". I didn't see her as vulnerable. I saw her as needing me there to support her no matter what, and that's what I was going to do.

Another moment was when she was in the hospital for an operation that required a 2 day stay in the hospital but turned into 5 days. I remember during this operation, which was a couple hours, I was worried, and I couldn't focus. I would think after all the chaos I saw, everything I been through, this is something where I felt helpless. I walked the halls of the hospital for hours, just praying for nothing to happen to her. I received a call from the doctors saying she was ok and that lifted a weight off my shoulders. When I could finally see her in the recovery room, I felt a sense of pain. It wasn't because she went through surgery, it was because she was in pain and I couldn't do anything about it. I saw her, she was barely awake, and she said "**I can't open one of my eyes**" (little did she know she had a reaction in the operating room so her eye was going to be swollen for a little while which the doctor explained to me in person). So when she said that I had to turn the other way because the way she said it I started to silently laugh. She was so out of it, not in pain, just curious. During this hospital stay was rough on me because I had to see the woman I would do anything to protect, to keep safe, in so much pain and I couldn't take her pain away, it killed me. I had to try to keep it normal and act like everything was fine. I kept a very stoic behavior, but deep down I was worried beyond words could explain. Lola, being her selfless self, always told me I looked uncomfortable on the hospital couch and I told her, "**No matter what you say, I'm not going anywhere and I'm staying here with you, So deal with it**." She hated it when I told her that, but it's true. True love doesn't go away when difficult times occur, it endures hard times regardless of the outcome. But during that time, it takes its toll on you, which I would take any day for her. I would always ask myself, "**Why her? After all the things I've done, why couldn't you just give that pain instead of her? I Know I deserve it, and I would do anything to take that pain away.** "

There's a profound clarity in moments like those—a stripping away of labels, doubts, and fears. What drives us to stay when others might walk away? Is it love, loyalty, or something deeper? I wasn't thinking about logic or expectations. My heart told me being there for her was all that mattered.

Lola once asked me when I realized I loved her. I gave her a lighthearted answer, trying to keep the moment casual, but I knew the exact moment. It was during a family gathering when my daughter, who had just met Lola, brought a puppy to her. Previously to this, my daughter saw Lola sitting close to me and she said "**That's My Dad**". So when she brought the puppy to Lola to show her, I could see something. I don't know how to explain it, but in my heart I saw a connection I've never seen.

Lola's face lit up as she interacted with my daughter, and something magical happened. My daughter, typically shy around new people, opened up to her as if they'd known each other forever. Their connection was instant and pure, and it moved me deeply.

At that moment, I didn't just love Lola for who she was to me—I loved her for the way she brought out the best in my daughter. She had the best ability to turn ordinary moments into extraordinary memories. She treated everyone with kindness, approached life with curiosity, and had a warmth that made people feel at home. Lola had a way to brighten the light to even the darkest room. Her smile and laugh was contagious, and in those moments I could truly see who she was, in her heart, at her core.

But as much as I loved her, there were always barriers. She held parts of herself back, as if afraid to fully let me in. Maybe it was her past. Maybe I wasn't the person she needed at the time. Whatever the reason, I never stopped trying.

What does it mean to give your all to someone who can't fully give it back? Is it a strength, a flaw, or both? These questions haunted me long after Lola and I parted ways. I gave her everything I had at the time or thought I had—not because I expected something in return, but because I believed in what we could have been.

Lola's presence was a balm for both me and my daughter. She brought a sense of calm and stability that allowed my daughter to thrive. And while my relationship with Lola eventually ended, the lessons I learned from her time with us remain. She taught me that building a family—no matter how unconventional—is about creating an environment of love, trust, and respect.

Lola wasn't just a love; she was a teacher. She showed me that love isn't about perfection—it's about persistence and showing up, even when it's hard. She reminded me that vulnerability is a strength, not a weakness, and that opening yourself up to someone is what makes love meaningful.

Loving Lola taught me to cherish the small times and remember those moments. It was those moments of vulnerability I loved those moments. When Lola would dance out of nowhere in the passenger seat while I was driving, she would start singing, claiming not to be able to sing, but her voice was so beautiful. It was seeing how she could never not be with her socks off, even though sometimes it was hot. It was when we would be next to each other, when she would put her foot on me, nudging me, then put her foot directly in front of my face. It was her way of telling me she wanted a foot massage. I would act like I don't see it, just to get a reaction out of her. It was moments where she was just herself, no makeup, no fancy clothes, no perfume, that she would catch me staring at her and call me a weirdo, but I was just stunned by her. It was seeing her smile, such an amazing organic smile unique to her. I loved it, and I always tried to make her laugh just to see it. She had a spicy personality, and I appreciated her in every way she was, the good or the bad.

Being with Lola was different. She would think that maybe I'd judge her if she was vulnerable, but I never did. She would think at times she would cry. She would think it was a sign of weakness, but I just told her "**It's ok,**" or she would call me crying and I would just listen. I would try to calm her down, but knowing her, once she's mad, you might as well stay out of her way because there is no calming her down until she's done. She would always be obsessed with her hair and used a bunch of hair products and sometimes, when she did use them, her hair would be all wild, according to her. I told her I loved it, anyway. She once asked me, "**Would I still love her if she lost her hair and went bald**?" and I told her, "**I loved her for who she was and not how she looked**."

Lola was an amazing shopper. She would always find a way to find the best sales or items at a great price. She was very good at managing money, too. There was a time she took a picture of my credit card and joked about how she was going to spend all my money. I told her I knew how she was, so I wasn't worried about it. So she bought something with my card when she was mad at me one time and didn't tell me. I got notified, so I knew, but I just didn't care. If it made her happy, that made me happy. I went to see her and while we were talking I said, **"So when were you going to tell me you bought something?"** In a joking way, she started laughing as did I. She said she bought it because she was mad at me and was waiting for me to say something, but I never did. I told her I saw it when it happened, but it didn't bother me.

There was another time Lola was mad at me, but she didn't know I booked a weekend getaway before she was mad. So I called her to tell her I was going to this getaway by myself and I would stop by her house on the way there. So I was able to convince her to come with me but she wanted to know where it was but I told her it was a surprise. She hated surprises. But I told her it was a few hours away but since we will be passing the beach we always go to, let's stop by and eat some food. I remember we would go to the beach. There was this beautiful hotel that was on the beach and we would always sit in front of it. That was our spot, and I remember telling her it would be nice to stay there one day. So when we arrived at the beach and while we were walking towards the food area on the beach, I changed directions. Instead of walking left, I turned right. I told her I needed to use the restroom, so I was going to use this hotel's restroom. She followed me and said they might not let me use it. But I said **"Yes they will since this is where we will be staying"**. I could see the look of shock and happiness on her face.

76

It was priceless. It was an amazing hotel room with a glass balcony directly on the beach, where we would leave the door open to hear the sound of the waves at night. Moments like that you will never forget.

She challenged me in ways no one else had. She was very blunt and didn't sway from telling the truth, showing me that true connection requires honesty, even when it's uncomfortable. She taught me that love isn't about fixing someone; it's about walking beside them as they navigate their challenges.

Through her, I saw a reflection of the man I wanted to be—the man I could be. She didn't just accept me for who I was; she inspired me to grow even if sometimes it hurt.

Even now, I sometimes wonder what could have been. If circumstances had been different, if we had met at a different time or under different conditions, could we have built a lasting life together? These "what ifs" linger, unanswered and unanswerable. But they don't diminish the love we shared. Not all loves are meant to last a lifetime; some are meant to teach us, to leave an indelible mark on our hearts. Lola was that kind of love for me.

▌LOVING LOLA: LESSONS UNFOLDED

Loving Lola taught me lessons I didn't know I needed to learn. Love, as I once believed, seemed all-powerful—capable of overcoming any obstacle, healing any wound, and bridging any distance. But my time with Lola reshaped that understanding. It showed me that love, no matter how deep or genuine, isn't always enough.

Sometimes, love serves as the foundation, but it cannot single-handedly hold everything together. It's a hard truth to accept, yet an essential one. The love Lola and I shared wasn't perfect, but it was real, and in its reality lay the profound lessons I carry with me today.

Even the most profound connections can falter under life's complexities. Yet, the importance of love doesn't diminish its meaning. The moments we shared, the lessons we learned, and the ways we grew together—that's the lasting legacy of our relationship.

Lola taught me that love isn't about perfection—it's about presence. It's about showing up, even when it's hard, even when you don't have all the answers. True love doesn't reside in grand gestures or fairy-tale moments. It lives in the quiet, messy realities of life—in shared silences, inside jokes, and the unspoken understanding that grows from truly seeing and accepting each other.

With her, I learned the power of vulnerability. To be vulnerable is to be brave, to let someone see the parts of you that you would rather hide. Lola had her walls, as I had mine, but at our best, we found ways to tear them down together. In those raw, unfiltered moments, we created something beautiful—something that, even if not permanent, was profoundly real.

But I wasn't the perfect man for her at the time, and I've come to terms with the ways I fell short. In my eagerness to give her everything she wanted, I sometimes forgot to give her what she needed. I believed love was about bending so far that I nearly broke, about saying "yes" to everything. But love requires balance. It's about giving and receiving in equal measure, about leading and following in harmony.

What Lola needed was someone who could provide both support and strength, which in my eagerness I failed to reveal the true warrior, supportive, and strong traits of who I truly am. She needed a partner who could lead her, but also let her take the reins when necessary. At the time, I didn't fully understand that. I wanted to make her happy, but in doing so, I may have unintentionally sent the message that I wasn't willing to take charge when it mattered.

For Lola, this chapter of our story may feel over. Perhaps she's closed the book, filed it away, and moved forward without looking back. She has always been resilient, adept at navigating life's complexities with strength and grace. And maybe she's right to do so. Perhaps she's found closure where I still seek answers.

The future remains a mystery. **Could our paths cross again? Could there be another chapter in our story?** Or was Lola meant to remain a poignant memory—a love that was, could have been, or could still be? What I do know is this: Lola will always hold a special place in my heart. She reminded me of my capacity to love deeply, to connect authentically, and to embrace vulnerability. She was a pivotal chapter in my life, one that shaped me in ways I'm still discovering.

But life rarely provides such clean endings. What feels final today might, in time, evolve into something new. Life has a way of resurfacing people and moments we thought we'd left behind. Just when you believe a door is closed, you might find a window cracked open, inviting you to revisit what lies beyond.

Or maybe this truly is the end. If so, I choose to honor what we shared by carrying its lessons forward. Rather than dwelling on what could have been, I focus on cherishing what was—and using it to guide me in the future. Rather than seeing my shortfall or what I could have done better, it taught me that improvement could always be needed, regardless of the situation.

▌ REFLECTIVE PAUSE

- **Have you ever experienced a connection so profound it felt destined?**
- **How do you reconcile the loves that don't last with the lessons they leave behind?**
- **Is it better to have loved and lost or to never have loved at all?**

Lola's chapter in my life may not have ended the way I hoped, but the lessons it brought were invaluable. Real love—transformative, life-changing love—is never wasted. It shapes us, strengthens us, and stays with us, even as we move forward into the unknown.

Some love stories aren't meant to have tidy endings. They remain open chapters, shaping us in ways we can't always predict. Lola's chapter in my life may have ended, but the lessons it brought will stay with me forever. I will not repeat the mistakes I made before. I will not take a step back, but control the situation. I will be the warrior, fighter and protector I am, but also love as much as I can. It made me realize taking control isn't about being controlling, it's about providing safety and reassurance when controlling is in a healthy manner.

Even now, I wonder about her. What is she doing? Is she happy? Does she ever think about what we had and what we could have been? These thoughts linger—not as regrets, but as reflections. As

I move forward. I carry the hope that the lessons I learned from loving Lola will help me become a better person, even in hard times. Pain from losing the one you truly love can be dramatic, but it can transform you if you use that pain as power to better yourself.

▌ REFLECTIVE PAUSE

- **What lessons have you learned from the people you've loved?**
- **How have those lessons shaped the way you approach love now?**
- **Have you ever let someone go, only to realize how deeply they shaped you?**

The love I shared with Lola wasn't perfect, but it was real. And even though it didn't last right now, or maybe it ran its course, it will always be a part of me—a reminder of what love can teach us and what it means to truly care for someone. At the end of the day, love isn't about holding on; it's about appreciating what you had and using it to grow.

Late at night, when the world quiets and my mind drifts unbothered, I often find myself revisiting the "what ifs." These are the questions that linger in the stillness, haunting the edges of my thoughts: What if we had found a way to make it work? What if we had chosen each other fully and without hesitation? What if the barriers that stood between us had crumbled beneath the weight of our love?

Would we have built a life together—a home brimming with peace, laughter, full of animals, family and the kind of love that endures the harshest storms? Or were we always destined to remain a fleeting story, a moment in time that burned bright but wasn't meant to last?

One memory always rises to the surface. It's a small, quiet moment, but it carries the weight of everything I felt for her. Lola once joked that she always fell asleep easily when she was with me, teasing that I must have sprayed something on the sheets. But it wasn't the sheets, and it wasn't the setting. It was us. It was the comfort we found in each other—the unspoken understanding that, in that space, there was no need for pretense or fear.

For me, those nights weren't just moments of rest; they were moments of peace, of knowing that I was exactly where I was meant to be. Yet, here I am, still grappling with the questions that have no answers. The "what ifs" are both a comfort and a torment. They remind me of what could have been, but also threaten to keep me tethered to a past that can't be rewritten.

How do you let go of the "what ifs"? How do you accept that some dreams will remain forever out of reach? These questions swirl endlessly, yet I know the truth: holding on too tightly to the past can blind us to the beauty of what lies ahead. Life isn't lived in the echoes of roads not taken; it's lived in the choices we make now and the possibilities we embrace moving forward.

▌ THE BEAUTY IN IMPERMANENCE

Not all love stories are meant to last a lifetime, and that's okay. Some loves are like shooting stars—brief but breathtaking, leaving a mark on your heart that glows long after the light has faded. Lola was my shooting star. She appeared at a time when I needed her most, illuminating the darkest corners of my life.

Even though our story didn't unfold the way I hoped, I can't regret a moment of it. There's a unique beauty in impermanence. It teaches us lessons we might not have learned otherwise, shaping us in ways we can't always foresee.

Loving Lola taught me to embrace vulnerability, to love unapologetically, and to find strength in the imperfections of life. She showed me that love isn't about grand gestures or fairy-tale perfection—it's about presence. It's about showing up, even when it's hard.

Have you ever loved someone deeply, knowing they weren't meant to stay? What did that love teach you? For me, Lola was a mirror. She reflected both my strengths and my flaws, challenging me to confront the parts of myself I had ignored. She helped me grow, and for that, I will always be grateful.

Lola was a chapter in my life, not the whole story. But what a beautiful chapter it was. Through her, I discovered parts of myself I didn't know existed—both the good and the not-so-good. She taught me that love requires balance, intention, and the courage to stand firm when it matters.

As I move forward, I carry these lessons with me. I've learned to approach love with a newfound awareness—to lead with strength while maintaining vulnerability, to communicate with clarity, and to never lose sight of my own identity in the process.

Not every love story is meant to last, but that doesn't make it any less meaningful. The moments I shared with Lola—our laughter, our quiet nights, our deep conversations—are treasures I will carry with me always. She was my teacher, my inspiration, and, in many ways, my peace.

Moving forward doesn't mean forgetting the past. It means integrating it into who I am, allowing it to shape me without letting it define me. Lola will always hold a place in my heart—not as a regret, but as a cherished memory.

▌ REFLECTIVE PAUSE

- **What chapters in your life have left the deepest marks on you?**
- **If you could speak to the people who were part of those chapters, what would you say?**

For me, if I could speak to Lola one last time, I'd say: Thank you. Thank you for teaching me how to love deeply and for reminding me of my capacity for connection. Thank you for the laughter, the lessons, and the moments of peace. You were my shooting star, and even though our paths diverged, you'll always hold a place in my heart.

At the end of the day, isn't life about collecting the moments and people who shape us, carrying them forward as we continue to write our story? Lola was a part of mine—a beautiful, unforgettable part—and for that, I will always be grateful.

CHAPTER 5

Personal Growth: Lessons in Love, Loss, and Resilience

Personal growth isn't linear—it's messy, nonlinear, and often uncomfortable. It's about peeling back the layers of who we are to understand why we act, react, and choose the paths we do. Growth requires a willingness to ask tough questions and sit with hard answers. It demands accountability, vulnerability, and a commitment to becoming a better version of yourself—not for others, but for yourself.

For me, growth has been about confronting my past, owning my mistakes, and recognizing the patterns that no longer serve me. It's not about perfection; it's about progress. It's about learning to love myself as I am while striving for who I want to be.

THE QUESTIONS THAT SPARK CHANGE

The toughest questions often lead to the most transformative growth:

- **Why do I react the way I do?**
- **What wounds from my past still influence my present?**
- **How can I break free from the patterns that no longer serve me?**

These questions have forced me to dig deep, often into the pain of my childhood. Growing up with the shadow of abandonment from my biological mother left scars I didn't fully understand for years. I internalized her absence as a reflection of my own inadequacy, believing that if I had been better, she might have stayed. But as I've grown, I've come to realize that her choices weren't about me—they were about her own struggles and limitations.

This realization has been both freeing and painful. It's allowed me to stop blaming myself, but it's also forced me to face the void her absence created. Growth means forgiving her, not for her sake, but for mine. It means releasing the blame I placed on myself and choosing to move forward.

Personal growth is often about breaking generational cycles. When you've grown up in an environment shaped by dysfunction—whether it's neglect, anger, or emotional unavailability—it's easy to carry those patterns forward. Recognizing those cycles is one thing; breaking them is another.

For me, breaking the cycle meant redefining what it means to love and provide. I used to think love was solely about sacrifice and provide because that's what I saw growing up. My father worked tirelessly to provide for us, but emotional connection was something we rarely discussed. I carried that same mindset into my relationships, believing that hard work and financial stability would be enough. It wasn't.

I've learned that love isn't just about what you give materially—it's about presence, vulnerability, and emotional connection. Breaking the cycle means doing things differently, even when it feels uncomfortable. It's about creating a new legacy for my daughter, one built on open communication, emotional availability, and unconditional love.

Growth begins with accountability. It's easy to blame others for your pain, but true change happens when you take responsibility for your own actions. For years, I blamed my ex-wife for the failures in our marriage. It wasn't until I stepped back and reflected that I realized I had played a role, too.

I wasn't as emotionally present as I could have been. I didn't assert myself when it mattered. I thought providing money for the bills was an act of love, but in doing so, I failed to lead with intention. Accountability doesn't mean taking all the blame; it means owning your part and committing to doing better.

LESSONS FROM LOVE AND LOSS

Relationships are one of life's greatest teachers. They show us our strengths, expose our weaknesses, and challenge us to grow. My marriage taught me the importance of staying true to myself. Changing who I was to fit someone else's expectations didn't make me a better partner—it made me lose sight of who I was.

With Lola, I learned that love requires balance. I wanted so badly to make her happy that I stepped back too much, leaving a void neither of us knew how to fill. Love isn't just about giving—it's about leading, supporting, and creating a space where both people can thrive.

Letting go of Lola isn't easy. It taught me that love can't be forced. You can give someone your heart, but you can't make them feel the same way. Letting go isn't failure—it's an act of self-love and trust in the journey ahead.

For a long time, I equated vulnerability with weakness. As a soldier, I was taught to push through pain without complaint. But I've learned that vulnerability is a strength—it's the courage to show up as your authentic self, even when it scares you.

In my relationships, I often avoided vulnerability, thinking it would protect me. But all it did was create distance. True connection comes from being open, from allowing yourself to be seen—flaws and all. Vulnerability is still something I'm working on, but I've come to see it as an essential part of growth.

Personal growth isn't a destination; it's a continuous journey. There will always be new challenges, new lessons, and new opportunities to grow. The key is to approach each step with intention, humility, and a willingness to learn.

For me, growth has meant facing the pain of my past, owning my mistakes, and striving to be better for myself and my daughter. It's meant breaking cycles, embracing vulnerability, and finding strength in accountability. It hasn't been easy, but it's been worth it.

▌ REFLECTIVE PAUSE

- **What does personal growth mean to you?**
- **What lessons have you learned from the pain and challenges in your life?**

For me, growth has been about finding the courage to face the hardest truths, forgiving myself for the things I couldn't control, and taking responsibility for the things I can. It's a journey I'm still on, but it's one I'm proud to be walking.

Growth isn't about becoming someone new—it's about rediscovering the strength, worth, and authenticity that's been within you all along. It's about taking the lessons life gives you, no matter how painful, and using them to become a better version of yourself. And in that process, I've found not just growth, but resilience, hope, and a deeper understanding of what it means to truly live.

▌ THE COMPLEXITY OF GROWTH

Personal growth isn't a straight line; it's a tangled web of setbacks, revelations, and progress. It's not about perfection but perseverance. Growth requires introspection, the courage to sit with discomfort, and the strength to own your mistakes. It's about peeling back the layers of who you are, challenging long-held beliefs, and continuously striving to become better—not for anyone else, but for yourself.

Too often, people avoid growth by running from the pain of their past. They leap into new relationships or distractions, thinking they can leave their struggles behind. But avoidance is temporary.

Without confronting the root causes of our actions, the same issues resurface, keeping us trapped in a cycle until we choose to break it. Growth demands bravery: facing the pain, examining the patterns, and refusing to shy away from the truth.

The way we respond to life's challenges is often rooted in the pain of our past. Parental trauma, neglect, or abandonment can leave wounds that shape our relationships and sense of self. For many, these early experiences create insecurities and fears that linger well into adulthood.

For me, my biological mother's absence created an emotional void that I carried for years. As a child, I questioned my worth, wondering if her leaving was somehow my fault. These thoughts planted seeds of inadequacy that took root deep within me. But as I grew older, I realized her choice to leave was not a reflection of my value but of her own struggles. It was never my burden to bear.

From that void emerged an unexpected gift: the love of my stepmother. She stepped into a role she didn't have to fill and became the mother I needed. Her love wasn't defined by obligation but by choice, and that choice taught me the power of connection and resilience. Her presence in my life was a reminder that pain often coexists with blessings. This duality—the hurt and the healing—became a foundation for my personal growth.

One of the most critical lessons I've learned is the importance of authenticity. In my marriage, I made the mistake of molding myself to fit what I thought my wife wanted. I changed the way I spoke, dressed, and even behaved, thinking it would strengthen our relationship. But in trying to become someone I wasn't, I lost myself.

Authenticity is the cornerstone of any lasting relationship. Pretending to be someone you're not may work temporarily, but it's unsustainable. Eventually, the real you emerges, and when it does, the relationship often crumbles. Looking back, I see that my efforts to be something I wasn't didn't bring us closer; they created a chasm between my true self and the person I was pretending to be.

The right relationships don't demand you to change your core. They celebrate who you are and encourage growth that aligns with your authentic self. I've learned that staying true to myself isn't just a personal value—it's a necessity for a meaningful connection. The right relationship brings out the best in each other regardless of the circumstances or difficult times.

Growth also requires vulnerability, a lesson I learned in my relationship with Lola. In my efforts to support her, I stepped back too much, letting her take the lead when I should have been more assertive. I thought I was being understanding, but in reality, I wasn't showing her the strength and confidence she needed. Sometimes you need to realize what went wrong, and how could it been different without becoming something you're not. It requires you to assess yourself and notice areas where you are falling short and work on those areas.

Vulnerability isn't about weakness; it's about courage. It's the willingness to be seen fully—flaws, fears, and all. It's about admitting when you're wrong, expressing your needs, and allowing others to do the same. My time with Lola taught me that vulnerability is the foundation of trust and intimacy. It's not always easy, but it's essential for genuine connection.

Growth often involves breaking the patterns we've inherited or created. For me, this meant confronting the ways my upbringing shaped my approach to relationships and fatherhood. I grew up equating love with being able to provide because that's what I saw. My father worked tirelessly to provide, but emotional connection wasn't something we talked about.

I carried this mindset into my relationships, believing that hard work and financial stability were enough to show love. But I've learned that love is more than provision—it's presence, vulnerability, and emotional connection. Breaking these cycles isn't easy, but it's necessary to create a healthier future.

Growth also means embracing the lessons life gives you, even when they're painful. The end of my marriage and my relationship with Lola taught me to value resilience, authenticity, and self-reflection. They showed me the importance of balance in love—of giving and leading, supporting and asserting.

Part of growth is learning to let go of what you can't control and forgiving yourself for what you didn't know at the time. Forgiveness isn't about excusing others' actions; it's about freeing yourself from resentment. It's about making peace with the past so you can move forward.

For me, forgiveness meant releasing the anger I felt toward my biological mother, my ex-wife, and even myself. It wasn't an easy process, but it was necessary. Forgiveness allowed me to reclaim my power and focus on building a better future. Remember, forgiveness isn't for the people that hurt you, it's for yourself.

Growth isn't about reaching a final destination—it's about embracing the journey. It's about finding meaning in the setbacks, learning from the failures, and celebrating the small victories. For me, that journey has been about reclaiming my sense of self, breaking unhealthy patterns, and becoming the person I want to be—not just for myself, but for my daughter and future relationships.

I've learned to balance ambition with contentment, strength with vulnerability, and effort with acceptance. Growth is about staying curious, remaining open to change, and trusting that every step— no matter how small—is part of the process.

▌ REFLECTIVE PAUSE

- **What patterns from your past are you ready to break?**
- **How has vulnerability shaped your relationships, and what does authenticity mean to you?**

For me, personal growth has been about embracing my imperfections, forgiving myself for my mistakes, and learning to stay true to who I am. It's a journey of resilience, self-discovery, and the unwavering belief that even the hardest lessons have something valuable to teach us. Growth isn't about erasing the past; it's about integrating its lessons into the person you're becoming. And that, I've come to realize, is the true beauty of this messy, unpredictable, and transformative journey called life.

CHAPTER 6

Emotional Intelligence: The Power Unseen

Emotional intelligence (EQ) is the quiet force that shapes our relationships, decisions, and personal growth. It's not just about naming emotions; it's about understanding where they come from, how they affect us, and how they guide the way we interact with others. EQ helps us make sense of life's messiness, showing us how to connect on a deep level, navigate conflict, and build trust.

For me, emotional intelligence has been a journey of trial and error. It's one thing to recognize your feelings, but another to handle them in a way that strengthens rather than harms your relationships. Learning how to balance what I feel with how I act has been a lesson that life keeps throwing at me—whether or not I'm ready.

At its heart, EQ is about two things: understanding your own emotions and genuinely connecting with others. It's what turns well-meaning words into actions that actually resonate. Think about how often you've said something with the best of intentions, only to have it come across completely wrong. Emotional intelligence helps bridge that gap.

Emotions have a strong impact. They can drive us to love deeply, create boldly, and fight for what matters—but they can also push us to lash out, shut down, or hold grudges. The hardest part isn't feeling emotions; it's knowing what to do with them. I've had moments where anger bubbled over, leading to words I regretted the second they left my mouth. Someone's frustration has also stung me, and I felt the pain of words not meant to hurt so much.

EQ doesn't mean suppressing emotions or pretending they don't exist. It means understanding them—asking yourself, Why do I feel this way?—and choosing how to respond. It's about finding the balance between feeling and thinking, reacting and reflecting.

One of the toughest lessons I've learned is how to pause before reacting. It sounds simple, but in the moment—when emotions are high and patience is low—it's one of the hardest things to do. I let my feelings control me, resulting in regrettable words and misjudgments, as I was too preoccupied with my emotions to see the whole picture.

But emotional intelligence has taught me to take a breath. To stop. To ask myself: What is actually happening here? Is my reaction going to help or hurt? The pause has saved me more times than I can count. It's not about bottling up emotions or pretending they don't exist—it's about giving yourself the chance to respond in a way you won't regret.

I won't lie—it's still a work in progress. There are times I fail, times I react before I think. But those moments have become fewer as I've learned to lean into that pause.

Emotional intelligence isn't just about handling your own feelings; it's about understanding others. This is where empathy comes in— the ability to see the world through someone else's eyes. It's about recognizing that most people aren't angry or upset for no reason. Often, there's a story behind their emotions—a fear, a worry, or a hurt that's driving them. A Lot of time's people assume they know what the other person has been through but never really know what they've been through.

I've learned that when someone lashes out, it's rarely about me. Maybe they're stressed, scared, or dealing with something I know nothing about. That doesn't make it okay, but it helps me respond with compassion instead of defensiveness. Empathy isn't easy. It requires listening—not just to the words people say, but to the emotions behind them. Sometimes, people don't need advice or solutions. They just need someone to hear them. Learning to listen in this way has been one of the most powerful shifts in my relationships.

EMOTIONAL INTELLIGENCE IN RELATIONSHIPS

EQ is the foundation of every meaningful relationship. Without it, small misunderstandings turn into big arguments, and unspoken feelings create distance. I've been in relationships where I lacked emotional intelligence—where I let my own insecurities and defensiveness get in the way of connection. Looking back, I can see how those patterns created cracks that eventually broke the relationship apart.

The hardest lesson I've learned is that emotional intelligence requires vulnerability. To connect with someone, let them see the real you—the fears, the insecurities, the emotions you'd rather hide. That level of openness can feel risky, but it's also where true intimacy is built.

In past relationships, I struggled with this. I thought being strong meant not showing emotions, not letting anyone see when I was hurt or unsure. But I've realized that real strength comes from being honest about what you're feeling and trusting the other person enough to share it.

Parenting has been the ultimate test of my emotional intelligence. Kids are emotional sponges—they pick up on everything, even the things you think you're hiding. If I'm stressed or frustrated, my daughter senses it instantly. If I'm calm and patient, she mirrors that back to me.

One of the most valuable tools I've learned as a parent is naming emotions. When my daughter is upset, I help her put words to what she's feeling: "Are you angry? Sad? Frustrated?" This not only helps her understand her emotions but also shows her it's okay to feel them. Naming emotions takes the mystery and fear out of them, making them easier to handle.

Parenting with EQ also means modeling the behavior I want her to learn. If I want her to approach challenges with resilience, I have to show her what that looks like. If I want her to treat others with kindness and empathy, I have to live those values myself.

Emotional intelligence isn't something you master—it's something you practice. I still have moments when I react impulsively or let emotions cloud my judgment. But the beauty of EQ is that it gives you the tools to reflect, learn, and do better next time.

One of the hardest parts of this journey has been unlearning old patterns. Growing up, I wasn't always taught how to process emotions in a healthy way. Like many, I learned to bottle them up, to "stay strong" and move on. But I understand that true strength lies in acknowledging your feelings—not ignoring them—and learning to navigate them.

Emotional intelligence has changed how I see myself, my relationships, and the world around me. It's helped me approach life with more empathy, more patience, and more intention. It's taught me that emotions are powerful, but they don't have to control me. I can choose how to respond, how to connect, and how to grow.

EQ isn't about being perfect—it's about being present. It's about striving to be a little better every day, for yourself and for the people you care about.

▍ REFLECTIVE PAUSE

- **How do you handle your emotions?**
- **How do you connect with the people in your life?**

For me, emotional intelligence has been a journey of mistakes, growth, and reflection. It's not about getting it right every time—it's about learning, adapting, and showing up with the best intentions. Because emotional intelligence isn't just a skill,—it's a way of being.

▌THE IMPORTANCE OF EMPATHY

What Is Empathy, Really?

Empathy is more than just a buzzword—it's finding how we connect with others on a meaningful level. It's about putting aside your ego and stepping into someone else's shoes, even when it's uncomfortable. It's not just about hearing what someone says but also noticing what they're not saying—the way their voice catches, the tension in their shoulders, or the moments they go quiet.

It requires effort to be empathetic. It means being present and tuning into someone else's world without judgment. It's about listening to understand, not to respond. You don't have to agree with someone to empathize with them, but you have to care enough to see things from their perspective. And when you do, it can change everything—relationships, conflicts, and even how you see yourself.

I've always prided myself on being observant, able to pick up on the little things—a shift in tone, a change in mood. I could sense when someone was upset or holding back. But noticing isn't the same as doing. I've learned that empathy isn't just about recognizing when someone is struggling; it's about stepping up to meet them where they are.

Looking back on my relationship with Lola, I can see how much empathy she needed. She was guarded, carrying pain she didn't always share. I thought being gentle and giving her space was the answer. I didn't realize that what she really needed was for me to lead, to be steady and present even when she couldn't say the words. I hesitated because I didn't want to overstep, but in trying to be careful, I missed opportunities to show her I could be her rock.

That experience taught me something big: empathy isn't passive. It's not just about understanding—it's about acting. Sometimes it's about being brave enough to step into a role you're unsure of because that's what the moment calls for. Empathy isn't just a feeling; it's what you do with it.

Let's be honest: being vulnerable is hard. It means showing parts of yourself you might not be proud of or admitting you don't have it all figured out. But I've learned that vulnerability isn't weakness—it's strength. It's what allows us to connect with others in a real way, to say, "I see you, and here's me, too."

Some of the most meaningful connections I've had came from moments of vulnerability. Whether it was admitting to my daughter that I didn't have all the answers or sharing my fears in a relationship, those moments broke down walls. They reminded me that people don't need you to be perfect—they need you to be real.

But vulnerability has to be genuine. You can't fake it. People can sense when you're not being authentic, and that can do more harm than good. True vulnerability is about showing up as you are, flaws and all, and trusting that it's enough.

Writing this—putting my experiences and lessons out there—is an act of vulnerability. It's not easy to admit where I've fallen short or what I've learned the hard way. But if sharing my story helps

someone else feel less alone, it's worth it. Vulnerability, I've found,
is the gateway to connection.

▮ TRUST IS BUILT ON EMPATHY

Empathy and vulnerability go hand in hand with building trust.
Trust doesn't happen overnight—it's earned, moment by moment,
through consistent actions. When someone feels truly seen and
heard, trust takes root.

I've seen this play out in my relationships. I showed Lola my
support by actively trying to understand her feelings. But I held
back on showing my own struggles, thinking it would make me
seem weak. What I missed was that trust isn't just about being
there for someone—it's about letting them be there for you, too. If
I had let her see more of my fears, it might have made her feel safer
sharing hers.

Empathy takes patience, too. People don't always open up on your
timeline. They carry their own fears and walls, and it takes time to
earn the trust that makes those walls come down. Empathy means
being steady, offering support without pressure, and showing that
you're in it for the long haul.

Empathy isn't just for deep relationships—it's something we can
practice every day. Whether it's with family, friends, coworkers, or
even strangers, empathy helps us navigate the messiness of human
connection. It's the key to resolving conflicts, understanding
different perspectives, and building stronger bonds.

As a parent, empathy has been one of my greatest tools. Kids act
out not because they're "bad" but because they're feeling something

they don't know how to express. When my daughter is upset, I try to help her name her feelings: "Are you angry? Sad? Frustrated?" It's a small thing, but it makes a huge difference. It shows her that it's okay to feel whatever she's feeling and that I'm there to help her through it.

At work or in friendships, empathy means listening—really listening—and trying to understand where someone is coming from. It's about asking questions instead of jumping to conclusions. Empathy doesn't mean you have to agree with everyone or fix everything, but it does mean you care enough to try.

Empathy isn't always easy. It can feel exhausting, especially when you're dealing with your own struggles. There have been times when I've been so caught up in my own pain that I couldn't see anyone else's. But what I've learned is that empathy creates a ripple effect. When you show someone understanding and kindness, it often comes back to you in ways you don't expect.

The hardest part of empathy, for me, has been setting boundaries. It's easy to pour so much into others that you forget to take care of yourself. But empathy doesn't mean losing yourself in someone else's world—it means balancing your compassion for others with compassion for yourself.

Empathy is something I try to practice every day. It's not always easy, and I don't always get it right. But I've come to believe that empathy is one of the most powerful tools we have—not just for connecting with others, but for creating a better world. It reminds us that everyone is carrying something, and a little understanding can go a long way.

For me, empathy isn't just about the big gestures—it's about the small, everyday moments. It's about listening without judgment, offering a kind word, or simply being present. It's about showing up, even when it's hard, and choosing to care.

▌ REFLECTIVE PAUSE

- How do you practice empathy in your life?
- How has it shaped your relationships or your understanding of yourself?

For me, empathy has been a journey—one of learning to listen, to act, and to be present. It's taught me that while we can't always fix someone else's pain, we can always choose to show up with kindness, patience, and an open heart. And sometimes, that's enough.

▌ NAVIGATING CONFLICT WITH EMOTIONAL INTELLIGENCE

Conflict Happens to everyone. Let's face it: conflict is unavoidable. It's woven into the fabric of every relationship—whether it's with a partner, a friend, a colleague, or even a stranger. And when emotions run high, things can get messy. You say something you don't mean, slam the door, or maybe shut down completely. That's the simple part—reacting without thinking. The hard part? Pausing, understanding, and finding a way to move forward without leaving scars.

Here's what I've learned: Conflict itself isn't the enemy. It's how we handle it that makes or breaks relationships. Emotional intelligence

(EQ) is like the cheat code for navigating conflict—not to "win," but to come out stronger on the other side. It's about choosing to understand over blame, connection over control. And trust me, it's a lot easier said than done.

Have you ever been in an argument where you say something in the heat of the moment and immediately regret it? I have. Those words hang in the air, and no amount of "I didn't mean it" can erase them. That's the thing about conflict—it's not just about what you say, but how the other person feels when they hear it.

EQ teaches you to slow down, take a breath, and think about what's really going on. Are you actually angry at the person in front of you, or are you projecting frustrations from something else? Is it the situation that's bothering you, or is it the tone of voice they used? Self-awareness is the first step in de-escalating conflict because it forces you to look inward before lashing outward.

One of the hardest lessons I've learned is that being "right" doesn't matter if the other person feels misunderstood. Communication during conflict isn't just about saying what's on your mind—it's about making sure the other person feels heard. And that starts with actually listening.

HERE'S WHAT ACTIVE LISTENING LOOKS LIKE:

1. Pay attention, not just to their words, but to their body language and tone.
   - Resist the urge to jump in with a rebuttal or a **"Yeah, but…"**

2. Acknowledge their emotions, understand their perspective, even if you don't agree with their perspective.

I used to think that listening meant nodding until it was my turn to talk. But I've learned that truly listening—sitting with their feelings and trying to see the situation through their eyes—can diffuse even the most heated arguments. Sometimes, people don't need you to fix the problem. They just need to feel like their feelings matter.

Let's be honest: apologizing isn't fun. Nobody likes to admit they messed up. But I've learned that a sincere apology can be the difference between repairing a relationship and watching it unravel.

The key is to own your part of the conflict without making excuses. Saying, "I'm sorry if you felt that way" shifts the responsibility onto the other person. Instead, try something like, "I'm sorry I hurt you. That wasn't my intention, and I want to make it right." It's uncomfortable, but it shows humility and prioritizes the relationship over your pride.

I used to think apologizing made me weak, but I've come to see it as a sign of strength. It takes courage to say, "I was wrong." And when you do, it opens the door for real healing.

Sometimes, conflict isn't even about you. The other person might be dealing with their own battles, and you just happened to be in the wrong place at the wrong time. With emotional intelligence, you can identify when someone's anger or frustration has deeper roots. It's about pausing and asking, "What's really going on here?"

One time, a close friend snapped at me over something I thought was stupid. My first instinct was to snap back—Dude, seriously? But I paused and asked, "Are you good? You seem really stressed?" That simple question shifted the whole conversation. They opened up about something they were struggling with, and suddenly, the conflict wasn't a fight—it was an opportunity to connect.

THE POWER OF THE PAUSE

Have you ever noticed how quickly an argument can escalate? One harsh word leads to another, and before you know it, you're both saying things you don't mean. That's where the pause comes in.

The pause is one of the most powerful tools EQ offers. It's that moment when you stop, breathe, and ask yourself:

Why am I reacting this way?

What am I trying to achieve in this conversation?

How can I respond in a way that brings us closer, not further apart?

It's not always easy. In the heat of the moment, it's tempting to fire back with a sarcastic comment or leave. But taking just a few seconds to gather your thoughts can completely change the tone of the conversation. It's not about bottling up your emotions—it's about channeling them into something constructive.

One of the hardest parts of navigating conflict is letting your guard down. Admitting that you're hurt, scared, or unsure takes guts. But vulnerability can transform conflict into connection. It shows the other person that you're not there to fight—you're there to work things out.

For example, instead of saying, "**You're don't take me seriously**," try, "**When you said that, it made me feel like my opinion or feelings don't matter**." That shift in language changes the focus from blame to your own feelings, which is much harder for the other person to dismiss. Vulnerability invites empathy, and empathy is the first step toward resolution.

Conflict is never fun, but it's one of the best teachers I've ever had. It's taught me to slow down, to listen better, and to value connection over being right. I've learned that people's actions are often reflect their own struggles, not a personal attack. And I've learned that sometimes, the best thing you can do is say, "I hear you. Let's figure this out together."

EQ has also taught me that conflict doesn't mean a relationship is failing. In fact, when handled with care, conflict can make relationships stronger. It forces you to communicate, to understand each other better, and to build trust by working through challenges as a team.

Conflict is a natural occurrence in life, but it doesn't have to leave a trail of destruction. With emotional intelligence, it can become an opportunity for growth, understanding, and deeper connection. The next time you find yourself in a conflict, try pausing, listening, and approaching the conversation with empathy and vulnerability. It's not about winning—it's about building something stronger together.

▌REFLECTIVE PAUSE

- **How do you handle conflict?**
- **Do you react in the heat of the moment, or do you take a step back to understand the bigger picture?**

For me, learning to navigate conflict with emotional intelligence has been a game-changer. It's taught me that real strength lies not in overpowering someone but in understanding them—and that's a lesson worth holding onto.

CHAPTER 7

Finding Peace

Sometimes, life feels like standing in the middle of a storm—everything spinning out of control while you're just trying to catch your breath. Finding peace in those moments isn't easy. It's not something you stumble upon or buy at the store; it's something you work toward, step by step, day by day.

For some people, peace comes from the quiet act of journaling—pouring their emotions onto a page and making sense of the noise. Others find it in meditation, prayer, or the comforting presence of a loved one. And for some, it's simply found in the decision to take one deep breath at a time. What I've learned is that peace doesn't look the same for everyone, and it's not a destination. It's a practice. For me, it's rooted in one of life's hardest lessons: acceptance.

Acceptance doesn't mean you're giving up or pretending the pain isn't there. It's not about being okay with everything that's happened. It's about saying, "This is my reality. Now what?" It's acknowledging that you can't change other people's choices, undo losses, or rewrite the past. What you can do is decide how you respond.

When people leave your life, it hurts. When someone you love walks away or lets you down, it stings. But acceptance has taught me to look at those moments differently. Instead of focusing on the people who left, I try to focus on the ones who stayed—the ones who value me, who show up, and who remind me of my worth. The people who walk away? Their absence, as painful as it may be, creates a space for something new, for someone better suited to stand beside you.

▌ THE PAIN OF LOSS

Loss has a way of reshaping you. It strips away your illusions and forces you to confront questions you may not want to face. During my deployments, I lost brothers—men who stood beside me in the trenches, who laughed and fought with me, and whose lives were cut short too soon. Their absence left an ache I carried for years, a gnawing sense of guilt and endless "what ifs." What if I had done something differently? What if I had been better, faster, stronger?

Eventually, I realized that no amount of second-guessing could change what happened. Acceptance doesn't mean the pain goes away; it means learning to carry it differently. It means honoring the people you've lost by living in a way that would make them proud. It means letting their memory inspire you rather than letting their absence consume you.

Loss isn't always about death. Sometimes it's about the absence of something you never had. As a child, I wrestled with the loss of my biological mother. She left when I was young, and for years I carried the belief that it was somehow my fault—that I wasn't enough to make her stay. That belief followed me into adulthood, coloring the way I saw myself and how I showed up in relationships.

It wasn't until much later that I began to understand her decision wasn't about me. It was her struggle, her story, her battle—not mine. In the void she left, my stepmother stepped in, showing me that love doesn't have to come from the people you expect. She didn't have to love me, but she did—and her presence became a reminder that family isn't always about blood. It's about who shows up.

Romantic relationships come with their own kind of heartbreak. When my marriage ended, it felt like a punch to the gut. I had poured everything into making it work, only to watch it unravel before my eyes. No matter how much you fight for someone, you can't make them stay if they've already made up their mind to leave.

And then there was Lola. Losing her hurt in a way I wasn't prepared for. With her, I felt something rare—a connection that made me believe in what could have been. But love, as powerful as it is, isn't always enough. People have their own wounds to heal and their own paths to walk. Acceptance meant letting her go, not because I didn't love her, but because I couldn't force her to see the depth of my love.

Maybe one day she'll look back and understand what she meant to me. Maybe she'll see the strength and care I poured into every moment we shared. But I can't live my life waiting for that day. Acceptance has taught me to move forward—to trust that letting go doesn't mean losing yourself. It means finding peace in knowing you gave your best at the time.

▌ REBUILDING AFTER THE STORM

Every loss, every heartbreak, every painful moment strips away something—but it also gives you the chance to rebuild. The process isn't about forgetting what happened; it's about taking those experiences and using them to shape something stronger. Each scar tells a story, and each story carries a lesson.

I've learned that rebuilding doesn't mean erasing the pain. It means finding a way to integrate it into who you are. It's about saying, "This hurt me, but it didn't break me." It's about choosing to grow, even when it's easier to stay stuck.

Acceptance isn't a one time decision. It's something you choose over and over again. It's deciding not to replay the past, not to hold on to bitterness, and not to let life's chaos steal your peace. It's about taking things one day at a time, trusting that even in the hardest moments, there's room for growth and healing.

For me, peace has come from learning to value myself—not based on other people's validation, but on my own integrity and strength. It's come from letting go of the need to fix everything and instead focusing on being present for the people who matter most.

Life will break your heart. That's inevitable. But it will also teach you how to rebuild. The people who truly love you will stay—not because they need something from you, but because they value who you are. And the ones who leave? Their departure is its own lesson—a reminder that you deserve relationships built on trust, respect, and mutual effort.

▍ REFLECTIVE PAUSE

- **What does peace look like for you?**
- **How do you find calm in the storms of life?**

For me, peace hasn't come from avoiding pain—it's come from embracing it, from learning to carry it without letting it weigh me down. Finding peace isn't about having all the answers—it's about trusting that, with time, you'll find your way. And maybe, just maybe, the chaos you're facing now will lead you to a strength you never knew you had.

▍ CHOOSING ACCEPTANCE: FINDING PEACE IN WHAT IS

What do you do when life feels like it's crumbling, when every breath feels heavy, and the question **"Why is this happening to me**?" keeps echoing in your mind. The answer isn't easy, and it's certainly not what we want to hear, but it lies in one simple and painful word: acceptance.

Acceptance doesn't mean pretending the pain isn't there or slapping a smile on when your heart is breaking. It's about standing in the storm, feeling every bit of the chaos, and choosing to face it rather than fight it. It's saying, **"This is my life right now, even if it's not what I planned."** It's not surrender—its strength. The kind of strength that allows you to move forward, one small step at a time.

The truth is, life doesn't come with guarantees or fair outcomes. We all know that, but it doesn't make it any easier to swallow. When something is ripped away—a dream, a relationship, a person—it's natural to cling to what could have been. You replay the moments, imagining a different ending, wondering if you could've done something, anything, to change the outcome.

But here's the thing: holding on to those "what-ifs" doesn't change the past. It only keeps you stuck in it. Acceptance is what allows you to release that grip and make space for something new. It doesn't erase the pain, but it softens the edges. It gives you the freedom to focus on what's still within your control—your response, your healing, your next steps.

One of the hardest parts of acceptance is understanding that some things are simply out of your hands. You can't make someone love you. You can't force people to stay. You can't go back and undo the past. Those truths can feel unbearable at first, but once you accept them, they can also be liberating.

I've learned that when someone chooses to leave—whether it's a partner, a friend, or a family member—it's not necessarily a reflection of your worth. Sometimes people have their own battles, their own paths to walk, and their choice to leave isn't about you at all. It's about them. That doesn't make the pain disappear, but it does shift the weight of responsibility off your shoulders. Their choice doesn't define you.

Forgiveness is one of the most misunderstood acts in the journey toward acceptance. For a long time, I thought forgiving someone meant saying, "Why should I be letting them off the hook for the hurt they caused?. I couldn't wrap my head around that. Why should I forgive people who hurt me?

But I've come to see forgiveness differently. It's not about them—it's about me. Forgiveness is about choosing to let go of the anger and resentment that keeps you tethered to the past. It's about freeing yourself from the bitterness that poisons your heart. It doesn't mean you excuse their behavior or let them back into your life. It just means you refuse to let their actions have power over you anymore.

Letting go of that anger is hard—sometimes it feels impossible. But holding onto it doesn't protect you; it only weighs you down. Forgiveness, I've learned, is the greatest gift you can give yourself.

Pain is inevitable. There's no escaping it. But the beautiful thing about pain is that it can be a powerful teacher if you let it. Every heartbreak, every loss, every disappointment carries a lesson. The trick is figuring out what that lesson is.

I've had my fair share of painful moments—the loss of loved ones, the end of my marriage, the heartbreak of watching someone walk away from a relationship I believed in. Each one felt like a wound that would never heal. But with time, I began to see the growth those moments forced me into. They taught me resilience. They showed me the strength I didn't know I had. They helped me set boundaries, value myself, and focus on what truly matters.

PAIN DOESN'T JUST TAKE—IT GIVES. ACCEPTANCE IS WHAT ALLOWS YOU TO SEE THE GIFTS HIDDEN IN THE STRUGGLE.

When life knocks you down, the idea of rebuilding can feel overwhelming. How do you start over when everything feels broken? The answer is simple but not easy: one step at a time.

Rebuilding isn't about forgetting what happened or pretending it didn't hurt. It's about integrating those experiences into who you are and using them to create something stronger. Every scar, every lesson, every memory becomes a brick in the foundation of the new life you're building.

You don't have to have it all figured out. You don't need a master plan. You just need the courage to take the first step, and then the next, and then the next. Over time, you'll look back and realize that piece by piece, you've created something beautiful out of the chaos.

FINDING PEACE IN THE CHAOS

Peace isn't about living a life free of struggle. It's about finding calm within the storm. It's about choosing to stop resisting the things you can't change and focusing on the things you can.

For me, peace has come from letting go of the need to control everything and learning to trust the process. It's come from forgiving myself for my mistakes and forgiving others for theirs. It's come from valuing the people who choose to stay and releasing those who don't. And most of all, it's come from accepting that life

will always have its ups and downs, but that doesn't mean it's not
worth living.

▌ REFLECTIVE PAUSE

- **What does acceptance mean to you?**
- **How do you let go of the things you can't control and
  find peace in the midst of life's chaos?**

For me, acceptance has been a hard-won lesson. It's not something
that happens overnight—it's a daily choice to let go, to move
forward, and to trust that even in the hardest moments, there's
room for growth, healing, and hope.

Life isn't about having all the answers. It's about finding the courage
to keep going, even when the path is unclear. And with acceptance,
you'll find the strength to take that next step. Always.

▌ THE BURDEN OF RESENTMENT

For years, I held onto resentment like a stone in my pocket. I
told myself I was justified—that the anger I felt was my armor,
protecting me from more pain. But the truth is, resentment doesn't
protect you; it imprisons you. It seeps into your thoughts, colors
your relationships, and keeps you tied to the very things you want
to leave behind.

At first, resentment feels empowering. It's like a flame you can
stoke when the pain feels too raw to face. It convinces you that
holding onto it will somehow right the wrongs or make the person

who hurt you pay. But here's the hard truth: they're not the ones paying the price. You are.

I didn't realize this for a long time. I thought that replaying the betrayals in my mind was my way of staying strong. But all it did was keep me anchored to the past, robbing me of the peace I so desperately wanted.

One of the deepest roots of my resentment was my biological mother. Her decision to leave when I was a child left a wound that longed for years. Every time I felt unworthy, abandoned, or broken, I traced it back to her absence. I built my resentment brick by brick, using it to construct a wall around my heart. It felt like protection, but really, it was a prison.

I wanted her to feel my pain. I wanted her to understand the depth of what her leaving had done to me. But the hard truth is, she didn't. And she likely never would. My resentment didn't change her; it only hardened me.

The breakthrough didn't come in a single moment. It wasn't a cinematic epiphany or a grand realization. It came quietly, over time, as I began to understand that her choice wasn't about me. It wasn't my fault. Her struggles, her decisions—they were hers alone. I couldn't rewrite the past or make her apologize for what I lost. But I could decide how much longer I would carry the weight of her choices.

Letting go of that resentment wasn't easy. At first, it felt like giving up the only thing tethering me to the pain. But slowly, I began to realize that forgiveness wasn't about excusing her or erasing the hurt. It was about freeing myself. Forgiveness was me saying, "**I won't let this define me anymore.**"

Forgiveness isn't simple, and it's certainly not instant. It's messy. It's uncomfortable. At first, it felt like I was letting her off the hook, as though forgiving her minimized the pain I'd carried for so long. But I came to see that forgiveness wasn't for her—it was for me.

Forgiveness is about breaking the chain. It's about refusing to let someone else's actions have control over your life any longer. It doesn't mean forgetting or pretending the pain didn't happen. It means deciding that you deserve peace more than you need to hold on to anger.

It took time. It took tears. And it took a lot of self-reflection to get to a place where I could say, "I forgive her," and truly mean it. But when I did, it felt like laying down a weight I didn't realize had been crushing me.

▌ FORGIVING YOURSELF

If forgiving others is hard, forgiving yourself can feel impossible. For years, I held onto guilt—guilt for mistakes I'd made, for relationships I couldn't save, for the ways I fell short. I replayed those moments, over-analyzing every choice and wondering if I could have done better.

Forgiving myself meant confronting my flaws and acknowledging my humanity. It meant recognizing that I was doing the best I could with what I knew at the time. It's not about erasing the mistakes but learning from them and moving forward with intention. Forgiveness doesn't just transform you—it transforms the way you interact with the world. When I forgave my mother, it didn't just give me peace; it opened my heart to deeper connections with others. The walls I had built around myself began to come down, and I found myself approaching relationships with more empathy, more patience, and more trust.

When I forgave myself, it gave me the courage to be vulnerable again. I stopped seeing my flaws as failures and started seeing them as lessons. I learned to approach life with hope instead of fear, and that shift changed everything. Forgiveness, it turns out, isn't just about letting go of pain—it's about making room for joy.

Resentment feels powerful, but it's a false power. It convinces you that holding onto it keeps you in control, but really, it controls you. Letting go of resentment doesn't mean the hurt disappears—it means you choose not to let it rule your life anymore. It's about saying, "I deserve better than this weight I'm carrying."

Forgiveness is a choice you make for yourself. It's not about absolving someone else or forgetting what they did. It's about freeing yourself from the chains of anger and bitterness. It's about choosing peace, even when the pain feels justified.

▌ REFLECTIVE PAUSE

- **What would it feel like to let go of the resentment you're holding onto?**

Imagine what it would be like to stop replaying those painful moments in your mind and start reclaiming your peace. Forgiveness isn't easy, and it doesn't happen overnight. But it's one of the most powerful gifts you can give yourself.

For me, the journey of letting go has been one of the hardest and most rewarding parts of my life. It's taught me that true strength isn't found in holding onto anger—it's found in choosing freedom. It's found in saying, "**This no longer controls me**." And in that choice, I've discovered a version of myself I'm proud of—a version that chooses love over anger, growth over bitterness, and peace over pain.

CHAPTER 8

Harnessing Pain as Power: Turning Struggles into Strength

Life has dealt me loss after loss, and there were times when I felt like the world was relentless, kicking me while I was already down. In those moments, it felt impossible to see beyond the hurt, as though the weight of the pain was too much to bear. But something happens when you hit rock bottom. A point comes when the pain doesn't feel as sharp, the blows don't break you the same way, and the fear that once haunted you start to dissipate. That's when you realize your true strength. It's not a revelation that happens overnight—it's born from enduring hardship and refusing to stay defeated. It's the moment when you stand up, look at the world, and defiantly say, **"Is that all you got, Ill take it all "**

Pain, in its rawest form, has the power to paralyze. But it also has the power to transform. The difference lies in how you choose to respond to it. Will you let it consume you, or will you harness it?

For me, the journey from pain to power wasn't linear. It was filled with setbacks, doubts, and moments when I wanted to give up. There were moments I didn't want to continue. I didn't want to love again to get hurt again. I didn't want to allow myself to become vulnerable because all I knew was pain. But through it all, I learned that pain can be a tool. It can be the fire that forges resilience, the fuel that drives ambition, and the catalyst for transformation.

Pain teaches lessons that no amount of success ever could. When you're at your lowest, you're forced to confront truths about yourself and the world around you. You see who's truly in your corner and who disappears when times get tough. You discover strength you didn't know you had, and you learn to appreciate the small victories that come with simply surviving another day.

For me, pain has been a constant companion. Whether it was the heartbreak of losing loved ones, the betrayal of people I trusted, or the crushing weight of my own mistakes, each experience has shaped me in profound ways. At first, I tried to ignore the pain, burying it deep inside and pretending it didn't exist. But that approach only delayed the inevitable. The pain would resurface, stronger than before, demanding to be faced.

Eventually, I realized that running from pain wasn't the answer. Instead, I needed to confront it, so I told myself "**Alright Motherfucker, since you're here might as well teach me something**" and I allowed it to let it teach me what I needed to learn. Every setback became a stepping stone, every failure a lesson, and every heartbreak a reminder of my resilience. Pain taught me patience, humility, and the importance of perseverance. It showed me that even in the darkest moments, there's a spark of light waiting to be uncovered.

There's a difference between someone who merely talks about resilience and someone who has lived it. When you've faced pain head-on and come out the other side, something shifts within you. **Fear no longer holds the same power. It doesn't paralyze you—it avoids you because it knows you're not easily shaken.**

Harnessing pain as power is about transformation. It's about taking the energy that comes from anger, sadness, or frustration and channeling it into something constructive. For me, this meant using my struggles as motivation to create a better future. Instead of letting my losses define me, I let them fuel me. I learned to stand taller, fight harder, and push forward with a level of grit that can only come from enduring the hardest of times. For me it's telling life **"After everything I've been through, After everything I lost , After all the pain I endured, Do you really think you can break me? "**

The process wasn't easy. It required me to confront my insecurities, face my fears, and accept that life isn't fair. But in doing so, I discovered a sense of purpose. I realized that my pain could be a source of strength, not just for me, but for others as well. By sharing my story and the lessons I've learned, I hope to inspire others to find their own strength in the face of adversity.

▌ REFLECTIONS FOR MOVING FORWARD

When we experience loss, it's natural to ask, **"Why me? Why now?"** But I've learned that these questions often have no satisfying answers. Instead, I've shifted my focus to questions that empower me: **"What can I learn from this? How can this make me stronger?"**

Loss is inevitable. Whether it's the loss of a loved one, a relationship, a job, or a dream, we all experience it in some form. But growth is optional. It's a choice we have to make, and it's not always an easy one. Growth requires us to confront our pain, to sit with it and let it teach us, even when all we want to do is run away.

HERE ARE SOME OF THE REFLECTIONS THAT HAVE GUIDED ME ON MY JOURNEY:

What have I learned from the struggles I've endured? Each challenge has taught me something valuable, whether it's the importance of resilience, the power of vulnerability, or the need to set boundaries.

How can I use my pain to build something meaningful? Pain has a way of clarifying what truly matters. It strips away the superficial and forces you to focus on what's essential. For me, this has meant prioritizing my relationships, my passions, and my personal growth.

Who do I want to become because of what I've been through isnt working? Pain has shaped me, but it doesn't define me. I've used it as a tool to become stronger, wiser, and more compassionate.

THE COURAGE TO REBUILD

Acknowledging loss is not about giving up—it's about finding the courage to rebuild. It's about standing in the ruins of what was and daring to dream about what could be. This process isn't linear, and it's not without setbacks. But each step forward, no matter how small, is a victory.

Rebuilding requires hope, even when it feels like there's none left. It requires you to believe in the possibility of a better future, even when the present feels unbearable. For me, this has meant redefining my goals, reevaluating my priorities, and committing to a path of growth and healing.

One of the most powerful lessons I've learned is that pain doesn't have to be permanent. It's a chapter in your story, not the whole book. By choosing to harness that pain and use it as a source of strength, you can write a new chapter—one filled with resilience, determination, and hope.

Peace doesn't come from avoiding pain—it comes from accepting it. It's about finding balance in the chaos and learning to navigate life's challenges with grace and resilience. For me, peace has come from understanding that I can't control everything. People will leave, circumstances will change, and life will throw curveballs. But what I can control is how I respond.

I've learned to find peace in the little things: the smile of my daughter, the quiet moments of reflection, the sense of accomplishment that comes from pushing through a tough day. These small victories remind me that even in the midst of chaos, there's still beauty to be found.

The journey from pain to power is never truly over. It's a continuous process of learning, growing, and adapting. There will always be new challenges, new losses, and new opportunities to harness pain as a source of strength.

As I move forward, I carry the lessons I've learned with me. I know that life isn't fair, but it's still worth living. I know that pain is a powerful teacher, and resilience is a choice. And I know that no matter what lies ahead, I have the strength to face it.

So, to anyone reading this who feels like the weight of the world is on their shoulders, know that you're not alone. Know that your pain doesn't define you—it's what you do with that pain that matters. Harness it. Use it. Let it fuel your journey. Because on the other side of pain is a strength you never knew you had. And that strength has the power to change everything.

CHAPTER 9

Warpath: Redefining Life's Battlefields

For years, I lived by the script society handed us. Work hard, stay loyal, pay your bills on time, and the rewards will follow—a steady career, a nice home, a comfortable retirement. It's the dream we're all sold, the promise that if we check off the right boxes, life will take care of the rest. But life doesn't always stick to the plan. When I was laid off, that small illusion crumbled. Suddenly, the formula didn't work. The stable path I thought I was on led straight to a dead end. I had to face a hard truth: the world I was prepared for didn't exist anymore. If I wanted to rebuild, I couldn't rely on outdated maps or familiar strategies. I had to change my mindset. I needed a new way forward. I needed a warpath.

"**Warpath**" might sound aggressive, even destructive. But for me, it's not about anger or conflict—it's about grit. It's about determination, resilience, and fighting for what matters most. It's waking up every day with purpose, even when life feels heavy. It's choosing action over excuses and progress over comfort. The warpath isn't just a mindset, it's a commitment. It's taking control of your life instead of waiting for someone else to fix it. It's saying, **"I'm responsible for my future, and I'll do whatever it takes to build it**." For me, that meant letting go of the idea that the world owed me anything. If I wanted security, I had to create it. If I wanted success, I had to earn it.

Walking the warpath isn't about ego or chasing empty achievements—it's about fighting for something bigger than yourself. For me, it's about providing for my family, building a legacy, and showing my daughter what perseverance looks like. Every time I think about quitting, I picture her. I imagine the home I want to build for her, the example I want to set. That vision keeps me moving forward.

Your warpath might look different. Maybe it's about pursuing a dream you've put off for years or proving to yourself that you're capable of more. Whatever it is, it has to mean something. The warpath is powered by purpose. Without it, it's just another road to burnout.

Let's be honest: the warpath isn't easy. It's exhausting. It means making sacrifices most people aren't willing to make. Long nights, early mornings, pushing through when every fiber of your being wants to stop. It's lonely, too. Not everyone will understand your drive, and some will even resent it. Relationships might strain, and self-doubt will creep in.

I've been knocked down more times than I can count. I've lost jobs, faced rejection, and battled insecurities that whispered, **"You're**

not enough." But each time I got back up. The warpath isn't about avoiding failure—it's about rising after every fall. It's about taking the lessons and turning them into fuel. It's about digging deep into yourself to say, "**Do you really think this is everything I got to offer? You haven't seen anything yet!**"

Success isn't glamorous—it's gritty. It's about doing the unglamorous work day after day, even when no one is watching. It's about staying the course when others give up. Most people want the rewards without the effort. They dream big but shy away from the sacrifices required to achieve those dreams.

The truth is, success belongs to those who outlast the setbacks. It's not about having the perfect plan—it's about showing up, doing the work, and refusing to quit. Talent might give you a head start, but persistence is what gets you across the finish line. Too many people decide they can't make a life for themselves and decide to just jump on the next person that has it, but it doesn't show their worth, it shows their vulnerability.

WHAT'S YOUR WARPATH?

Here's the question that changed everything for me: **What am I willing to fight for**? If you don't have an answer to that question, life can feel aimless. But when you do, even the hardest battles start to feel worth it. In a warpath, you have to become an animal. You have to tell yourself nothing will stop me. **I told myself after all the hurt that has been done to me, nothing is going to stop me from getting what I want. The world is going to feel my wrath!**

Your warpath doesn't have to be grand. It might be about improving your health, creating financial stability, or rekindling a relationship.

What matters is that it's yours. It's a path that reflects your values and moves you closer to the life you want. You have to stay on course even when it gets hard, and trust me, it will. It will test your inner being, but instead of hiding it, embrace it.

The warpath is long, and there will be times when the weight feels unbearable. On those days, it's easy to lose sight of why you started. That's when you need to lean into your "why." For me, it's my daughter. It's the promise I made to myself to create a life I can be proud of. When the road gets hard, I remind myself of that promise, and it pushes me forward.

Staying on the warpath requires discipline. It means cutting out distractions and surrounding yourself with people who believe in your vision. Not everyone will support you, and that's okay. You have to also ask yourself, Who's with me and Who's Not? The warpath isn't about pleasing others—it's about staying true to yourself.

The rewards of the warpath aren't just about material success. Yes, there's pride in achieving your goals, but the real reward is what you become in the process. The warpath teaches resilience, discipline, and the power of perseverance. It shows you that you're capable of more than you ever imagined.

Final Thoughts

The warpath isn't for everyone. It's demanding, relentless, and sometimes isolating. But for those who choose it, it's also empowering. It's a reminder that you're the author of your own story and that you have the strength to overcome whatever life throws your way. For me, it's about creating what I want, taking what is mine, and showing the world nothing is going to stop me. After everything I have been through, Do you really think you can stop me? Do you really think I'm out for good? **I'M JUST GETTING STARTED**. When people break under pressure, **I DON'T**, When people run away from hard times, **I DON'T**, When people think they got the best of me? **NOT EVEN CLOSE**.

So, ask yourself: **What's my warpath? What am I willing to fight for, sacrifice for, and endure for?** Once you find your answer, commit to it with everything you've got. The journey won't be easy, but the destination will be worth it. Stay focused, stay disciplined, and keep pushing forward. The warpath is yours to walk—make it count.

A Journey of Resilience, Growth, and Purpose

Looking back on my journey, I see a mosaic of pain, perseverance, and transformation. The person I once was—the one weighed down by loss, heartbreak, and self-doubt—could never have imagined the strength I've discovered within myself. Each challenge, whether it came in the form of deployment, the unraveling of a marriage, or the burden of personal struggles, became a stepping stone toward growth. And while the scars remain, they tell a story—not of defeat, but of survival and resilience.

If there's one truth I've come to understand, it's that life will never be fair. It will knock you down when you least expect it. It will test you, break you, and leave you questioning your worth. But life will also give you opportunities to rise—to rebuild, to learn, and to become more than you ever thought possible. The power to transform your pain into purpose lies within you. That's a lesson I've carried with me every step of the way.

For years, I allowed the expectations of others and the weight of my failures to define me. I tried to fit into molds that were never meant for me, to chase a version of happiness that wasn't my own. It wasn't until I embraced the chaos, the uncertainty, and the pain that I found clarity. I learned that true strength comes from within—from accepting yourself as you are and striving to become the person you're meant to be.

This journey has also taught me the value of forgiveness—not just for others, but for myself. I've let go of the resentment that once consumed me, releasing the grip that pain and anger had on my soul. Forgiveness isn't a sign of weakness; it's a declaration of strength. It's choosing peace over bitterness, growth over stagnation, and love over fear. And while forgiveness takes time, I've realized that it's one of the most liberating acts of self-love a person can practice.

FAMILY: THE HEART OF MY JOURNEY

To my Daughter: You are my light, my beacon of hope—the one constant that keeps me moving forward even when the world feels impossible. From the first moment I held you, my purpose shifted completely. Every sacrifice, every moment of doubt, and every ounce of strength I have poured into my life has been because of you. You've taught me more about love, hope, and resilience than any hardship or challenge ever could.

My greatest hope is that when you read this book someday, you'll understand how deeply I love you and how much you've inspired me. Life will challenge you. You'll face defeats, heartbreak, and moments of doubt. But if this book teaches you one thing, it's that you can overcome anything.

The journey I share here isn't perfect—it's filled with mistakes, regrets, and moments I wish I could change. But it's also full of lessons, growth, and resilience. I hope my story gives you the courage to face your challenges head-on. Always remember: you have a father who loves you unconditionally and believes in you endlessly. No matter what happens, I'll always be in your corner, cheering you on.

To My Dad: You've been one of my greatest teachers. Even when we didn't see eye to eye, your example taught me the value of hard work, standing tall, and facing life with resilience. You showed me that strength isn't just about physical toughness, but moral courage, emotional endurance, and continuing on when the odds feel impossible.

Your lessons have shaped me, guiding every step of my journey. This book reflects your influence as much as it does my experiences. Thank you for your sacrifices, your wisdom, and your love—even when it wasn't spoken aloud. This book is my way of saying thank you—for being my guide, my rock, and my father.

To Amanda and Kat: my sisters, you have been my constants in a world that often feels chaotic and uncertain. Amanda, your unmatched strength and determination inspire me. The challenges you've faced would break most people, but you've always risen with grace and resilience.Kat, you've been my balance, my partner in mischief, and my mirror. You remind me to laugh, take life less seriously, and find joy even in the hardest moments. Together,

135

you've both taught me what unconditional love, unwavering support, and staying connected mean—even when life pulls us in different directions. This book is for you—a tribute to our bond and the strength you've given me.

To Lola: You were a bright and beautiful chapter in my life. Like a shooting star, your presence was brief, but left an indelible mark on my heart. You taught me lessons about love, vulnerability, and the beauty of fleeting moments. In time you will see who I truly am. Although our paths have diverged, I hold on to the warmth of the love we shared and the lessons you brought into my life. You always said i couldn't handle you but that is far from the truth.

To Lola's Children: Life will get tough, life is relentless but never give up. Set out for your goals and remember you're never alone. Even in moments of distance, it wasn't because I didn't care—it was because I didn't want to disappoint you both. Know that you both will always hold a special place in my heart. Always be yourselves, and if you ever need anything I'll always be here for you both unconditionally.

Lola's family: who welcomed me as one of their own, thank you. Your kindness and acceptance meant the world to me. You are all a part of my story, and I will always be here for you, no matter where life takes us. Lola's brothers, sisters, and parents—my eternal gratitude and love. Family isn't just about blood; it's about the bonds we choose to honor and nurture.

To My Family and Those Who Supported Me To my family and everyone who stood by me through my hardest times, thank you. You've been my foundation—the steady ground beneath my feet when everything else felt like it was falling apart.

Through a kind word, a helping hand, or simply your presence, you reminded me that I was never alone. Your love and encouragement have been my lifeline, and I hope this book serves as a testament to the power of family, resilience, and unconditional love.

MOVING FORWARD

As I move forward, I carry these lessons with me to become an unstoppable force the world will see. I know there will be more challenges ahead, more moments of doubt, and more opportunities to grow. But I also know that I'm ready. The warpath I'm walking, the pain I've endured, and the strength I've discovered have prepared me for whatever comes next. This isn't the end of my story—it's the beginning of a new chapter, one written with intention, purpose, and an unshakable belief in my ability to overcome.

TO THE READER

To you, the reader, thank you for walking this journey with me. If there's one thing I hope you take away from my story, it's this: You are stronger than you realize. Your pain doesn't define you—how you rise from it does. Life will test you, but those tests are opportunities to discover your resilience, your purpose, and your power.

So, as you turn the page and begin your own next chapter, remember that you have the strength to keep going. Embrace the chaos, find peace in the storm, and never stop fighting for the life you deserve. This is your story—write it boldly, authentically, and unapologetically.

FINAL THOUGHTS

The journey of resilience, growth, and purpose is never truly over. It's a constant process of learning, adapting, and striving to be better. Through the ups and downs, the love and loss, the victories and failures, I've learned that life is about more than just surviving—it's about thriving. It's about taking the lessons from your past and using them to build a future filled with hope, love, and intention.

To my family—both by blood and by heart—you are my reason to keep pushing forward. And to anyone who reads these words, know that you are not alone in your struggles. You have the power to rise, to rebuild, and to create a life that reflects the person you are meant to be.

Thank you for being part of my journey. Now, go and write the next chapter of yours.

Made in the USA
Middletown, DE
28 January 2025

70480790R00084